Dew Drops

SPEAKS ABOUT YOU

VEMURI BALARAM

PUSTAK MAHAL®
Delhi • Mumbai • Patna • Hyderabad • Bangalore

Publishers
Pustak Mahal®, Delhi

J-3/16, Daryaganj, New Delhi-110002
☎ 011-23276539, 23272783, 23272784 • Fax : 011-23260518
E-mail : info@pustakmahal.com • Website : www.pustakmahal.com

Sales Centre

10-B, Netaji Subhash Marg, New Delhi-110002
☎ 011-23268292, 23268293, 23279900 • Fax : 011-23280567
E-mail : rapidexdelhi@indiatimes.com

Branch Offices

BANGALORE : ☎ 080-22234025
E-mail : pustak@sancharnet.in • pmblr@sancharnet.in

MUMBAI : ☎ 022-22010941
E-mail : rapidex@bom5.vsnl.net.in

PATNA : ☎ 0612-3094193 • Telefax : 0612-2322719
E-mail : rapidexptn@rediffmail.com

HYDERABAD : Telefax : 040-24737290
E-mail : pustakmahalhyd@yahoo.co.in

Dew Drops

SPEAKS ABOUT YOU

First Published : 2006

Translated from Telugu to English by
Dr. J. Bhagya Lakshmi

ISBN 81-223-0949-6

Printed at : Sri Industries Offset Printers,
B-116-117, Sector-II, Noida (U.P)

To

My companion and guide,

My whole and soul,

The One who took all the sufferings as her share,

And distributed joys and comforts as my share,

My best-half, my life-partner

Smt. Ammaji Balaram

I dedicate this work.

Vemuri Balaram

Before it Rains...

SWATI, the Largest Circulated Telugu Weekly with a readership of 39.59 lakhs, carried the Editorials with the title 'SWATI CHINUKULU'. They struck an instantaneous bond with its readers as evidenced by the mail that thronged the HO of Swati week after week.

These nuggets of wisdom from the Creative Genius Sri Vemuri Balaram, the Founder and Editor of SWATI, made a deep impact with a philosophical yet pragmatic and comprehensive yet compact style.

These thoughts based on the author's analysis of men and matters are simple, easy to grasp- yet profound! Using wit and wisdom,he provides practical insights into the true path of life through the application of timeless principles supported by his bedrock character.

These philosophical musings by Sri Vemuri Balaram, the TANA TELUGU MAGAZINE MOGHUL AWARDEE, are loaded with hope, direction, encouragement and beliefs in the well-being of the mankind.

Sri Vemuri Balaram vouches that what the society today needs is not just great personalities but good and benevolent people. The qualities of the good and the evil were discussed in a lucid manner for the delight of all the members of the family- the children, the youth, men and women, who await the release of SWATI, week after week.

We are honoured and delighted to present the English rendition with the title 'DEW DROPS' which sets out a code for better living with its focus on self-improvement and core human values.

It is hoped that this good work by Sri Balaram, the Trend Setter and Master Craftsman in Telugu Magazine Journalism, will continue to inform and inspire readers in their pursuit to become good men who are fully human and fully alive.

Publishers

Friendly Musings

Vemuri Balaram - The Precious Pearl in the Telugu Household.

In the sky, Swati is - The Laughing Star

In the nature, Swati is - Ecstasy-filled Season

In Horoscope, Swati is - The Haven of Precious Gems

Among Weeklies, Swati is - The Running Queen.

Balaram-wields the pen as plough and tills the field of columns. Swati-rains 'Dew Drops' and grows a bumper crop of pearls.

Telugu land is the farmer's land. Swati Weekly is the weekly edition of the timely rains. Like a star, Swati shines and glows in the eyes of the readers.The expectant eyes of the ever enthusiastic and curious reader await the arrival of Swati. Fully illustrated cover page, variety-filled decoration of art and drawings, from sensuous feelings to feelings of the sensual restraint, life in its myriad ways and various forms fully animated and made lively with the beautiful play of navrasas- with all this and more, Swati delights the Telugu readers who are served delicious dishes on a platter.

All the pages in Swati stand on one pedestal!

As Dew Drops, Balaram's Editorial stands on another high pedestal!

The rain drops in nature fall into the fields and touch the soil resulting in a special fragrance as a precious gift to our sense of smell. Balaram's Swati Chinukulu (Dew Drops) in the weekly give a loving warmth to the barren and dry hearts in the field of life radiating on them the fragrance of humanity.

That Dew Drop-The friendly touch of a perspiring cloud.

This Dew Drop-The sprouting of an endearing heart.

That Swati-The Merciful One, shedding tears as gift for the dry land.

This Swati-The Virtuous One's gift of perfumed water to the barren and dry souls.

And so, Balaram's 'Dew Drops' are soothening and mellifluous songs touching the hearts of Telugus. The drops rain in Swati, stay in the reader's heart and remain forever delighting them as precious pearls.

On a weekly basis, Sri Vemuri Balaram has served us a bag of pearls and gems which we can take into our possession.

As the name of Swati is so naturally beautiful, its feature 'Dew Drops' is ever so austerely wonderful. The solid cloud's quest for becoming liquid results in the life-giving source- a drop of water. In the same way, 'Dew Drops' are the tales of experience of Balaram's heart deeply touched and melted by the solidified and smoke-filled clouds of joys and sorrows, riches and poverty found in the lives of the people.

Every single page article is a friendly soul talking from a shining oyster!

Balaram doesn't discuss politics, but rips the cruel and dirty games of politics apart. Balaram doesn't preach morals, but points out the corruption and sets the system straight. Balaram doesn't stab you with a pen by telling you cock and bull stories, but he ensures the inculcation of the morals that should withstand the test of time. He doesn't make fun of anyone, but smilingly sets the things in order. He doesn't turn an editorial into a book of proverbs just for the fun of creating proverbs, but he makes us remember the good words that help us lead our life forward. He doesn't write poetry but fills his writing with novel concepts.

Balaram's pen tills the land, draws the lines in the field of life and sows the seeds of the present for a better future. It sieves out the legion of experiences and makes them sprout and blossom in our hearts.

Balaram tills the land and works hard for a great crop and the readers enjoy the rich harvest. And so, 'Dew Drops' are the words giving wake up call to the Telugus to enter the path of light and truth!

Balaram is the sculptor who carved raindrops into precious pearls. Every pearl has its lustre. Every article in this book is a pearl. In every article, the turban (the heading) is the first flash of lightning, the girdle is the second one and the conclusion is the third and final flash of lightning and lustre.

The flash of lightning associated with the heading is like a crown of precious stones and gems. The lustre of middle paragraphs beautifies the look of the article like the girdle. The conclusion is full of lustre as it has a proverb or a sympathetic and sensitive advice which touches the reader and outshines everything else. It benefits everyone, comes close to the reader's heart and remains in reader's mind forever.

This is the first rain of 'Dew Drops'. I do hope that many more rains will come down. The drops of Swati should continue to remain as a gift to every member of the family, week after week. The silent song sung by this 'Dew Drops' is- "It is our responsibility to sow good seeds" and "We have to do good to others as we wish to do good to ourselves".

This is the Good News! The Great Psalm! The Path of Life being Trodden by Sri Balaram!

(G.V.Subrahmanyam)
Former Vice-Chancellor
Potti Sri Ramulu Telugu University

CONTENTS

INVITATION

We celebrate many auspicious occasions like marriages, house warming among others. We invite relatives, friends and well wishers to attend the functions. The invitations are extended with a view that all will get together on these occasions.

But gradually all these functions are limited to exhibitionism.

We think the more people we invite,the greater the function would be.

Having invited them, we don't even have time to greet and say hello to the invitees. The invitee himself has to go to the host to say,"Here I am" and mark his presence felt.

It is not nice not to invite. So invitation is extended. It is not nice not to attend. So one attends the function. Everyone knows that love and affection are non-existent. Since too many people are invited,neither the hosts nor the guests are comfortable.

And it is not surprising if there is a stampede at the food counters.

These invitations, dinners exceed all limits and result in wasteful expenditure. Under the present circumstances, all these need to be controlled.

If the increased expenditure leads to debts, that cannot be termed as celebration. This tradition should change.

When we celebrate, let us invite only that number of people whom we can afford.

This is beneficial to both. Once this method is followed, celebrating auspicious occasions becomes meaningful.

IN OUR HANDS

At times we tend to complicate very simple matters. Those which can be easily resolved become insoluble because of our own doing.

For example :

We have all the facilities to send an important letter or anything by mail. There are facilities like registered post, courier service etc... But we do not care to make use of them.

If we want to send a thing to a person in some other town, what many of us do is to hand it over to a friend or someone else who is visiting that place requesting him to hand it over to the addressee.

If they can do this, it is fine. But what if that person loses the thing on the way or hands it over to someone else by mistake, or he forgets to do the needful because he is preoccupied? All these can happen. In the meantime, we are so tensed up that we start calling them on STD or Trunk call enquiring. "Have you received it? I sent it through such and such a person."

After all this, does it reach them in time without any problem? It is doubtful. So a work which could have been easily done through post is turned into a complicated problem unnecessarily.

In the bargain, our time as well as the time of others is wasted. We lose our peace as well.

If we make use of the services properly to the maximum extent possible, that is good for both the parties and is no trouble for the third person.

NO SCALES TO WEIGH A PERSONALITY

Everyone thinks that he has a certain status. Some think their intellect is different. Some others think their position is different. There are yet others who think their status is different. They also live accordingly.

They befriend or develop relations only with people of their level. They don't allow others below their level come anywhere near them.

When it comes to children there too we divide them saying one is bright in studies and another is not so bright. Today's teachers are also dividing the children similarly.

Teachers boast that their students are those who get cent percent marks. Some universities are open only to merit students. If someone is already intelligent and skillful what is there for us to teach them.

Even if we want to shift a child from one convent school to another convent school he has to face tests.

A student of the fourth standard is given admission in the first standard. They justify themselves saying the child may not be able to compete with other students and thus suffer from inferiority complex. So they are trying to help the child for his own good.

If we see history we understand that the one who faced humiliation and ridicule alone is proving himself to be great. The one with anger, diligence and dedication can achieve anything. If one is associated with the people of his own status he will remain one among the many and cannot have a goal of his own. Let us congratulate those who are different. Let us fling off the touchstone called status.

UTILISATION IS IMPORTANT

We have to learn everything ever since we are born. It does not mean everyone should know everything and be talented in every field.

Everything requires skill. One who knows the subtlety of the work goes forward. The one who does not know remains where he is.

Those who continue to learn new things realise at one point of time that they have adequate knowledge about everything. By then they see age is catching up.

Then the body does not cooperate, mind loses its sharpness to put into practice all that has been reaped so far. So even though we are capable we are not in a position to do many things.

What we should do is to make use of our learning however limited it may be. Our thoughts and experience should take shape in deeds.

Only then a person can see the fruit of one's effort and can enjoy it. However learned one may be there is always much more to learn and to know.

Once a disciple went to his teacher and told him that he learnt how to fly in the air after twenty years of relentless practice. Then the teacher replied, "You wasted twenty years of precious time in your life just to achieve what a little bird can do with ease."

So whatever we learn should be useful to us as well as to society. Instead of moving ahead acquiring endless knowledge it is better to put into practice the limited knowledge one has acquired. Then life does not remain incomplete. One has the joy of living life to the full.

AIRTIGHT PLACE

Before a marriage is settled both the parties of bride and bridegroom should talk over matters. They can ask for any details they require from each other.

They can discuss matters and can even challenge each other because both have courage and boldness to search for another alliance if not this. Only when both the parties agree the auspicious time for marriage is fixed.

But actual trouble starts neither before the marriage nor during the marriage. It starts the moment the marriage is solemnized.

Everyone is in one's own limits and everyone has one's own position. Now that the marriage is over each one thinks he is high and mighty. Bride's people should tread cautiously. They have to deal with the bridegroom's people in a very polite way. Otherwise words are exchanged and conflicts take place.

In fact the marriage should strengthen relations. On the contrary why are they becoming weak?

It is surprising but true. It is necessary to handle all dealings delicately. Then only the relations between the both parties will be smooth or else they will be strained.

Sometimes we doubt whether marriages with this kind of strained relations are good. In fact the relations should be so strong that a third party has no chance to interfere.

Then no one can defy the other. When marriage brings two people together the alliance should bring two families together. That is a true marriage alliance.

THAT IS WHY THERE ARE FOUR DIRECTIONS

Every person has his own style. He does everything the way he likes. Some people have great speed. Others are slow. There are people who are in between. So we have a variety of personalities.

It may sound funny but our acts appear to be ridiculous to other person. So also the other person's acts look crazy for us. So it is inevitable we find fault with each other and criticise each other.

Even every day routine work is also done differently by different people. Starting with the brushing of teeth till one retires to bed everything is done differently.

Even in one family each one gets up from bed at different time. So also they sleep at different time. From all this we understand that every person lives according to his will and each one has his style.An individual can do the work he likes most effectively.

Even if we want to do something or want to get something done we should know what we like. Similarly we should find out what work the other person can do well. If we entrust a person with the work he can shoulder he can give the best results. When we ourselves do not know what we want or what we need we encounter only defeat. If we ourselves are proceeding in chaotic style we cannot hope to get anything from others.

The day it is clear what we want to achieve and what our goal is there are many brilliant people who can be of help to us.

Thus every individual has his own liking and the one who follows it alone can be a winner.

IN GOD'S PRESENCE

I am talking about theists who have faith in God. Nothing to bother about atheists.We visit temple to have a glimpse of God. We take the trouble of going all the way to Yadagiri Narasimha Swami, Tirupati SriVenkateswara Swami or Vijayawada Kanaka Durga for seeking their blessings.

But having gone there, do we really watch the Lord at sanctum sanctorium? Are we able to imprint that image of the Lord of Universe on our heart? To a great extent, we fail to do that.

When we are before the Lord, we close our eyes, slap our cheeks and join our palms in all humility If possible, we would like to prostrate before God. Then we recite our list of demands. In the meantime, it is time to leave and unceremoniously we are asked to move. We come out of the temple with a heavy heart. The root cause of all this is our inability to see the Lord with open eyes to our heart's content.

We can as well slap our cheeks and pray to Him with closed eyes at home itself. Then why did we go that far just to do the same?

Doesn't our Lord know what our desires are? Should we specially bring them to His notice? He knows our requirements. He Himself will arrange everything for us in time.

So, when we visit a temple next, let us not close our eyes. Within that limited time, let us see the Lord to our heart's content.

FRIENDSHIPS WITH SET PURPOSES!

Friendship in childhood is naive and unadorned. Friendship that is formed in later years has more colour glasses and masks.

The foundations of childhood friendship are sweet. There is neither a need to understand each other, nor an opportunity to do so.

Yet-those feelings are different.

One makes friends in later years also. But only a few remain as close friends.

When one grows up, one is in a position to understand the other person. So in adulthood the friendship that is formed between two individuals with proper understanding lasts for ever. But the friendship with a set motive has a brief life span.

Unfortunately, in the persent world there are only a few genuine friendships and a number of contacts based on necessities. Now friendship is not based on affection. The necessities are the measuring scales of friendship.

There is a difference between acquaintances and friends. Close friends come under some other category. To a great extent, we consider the acquaintances around as close friends and get along with life.

These friendships are broken as soon as they are made once the need is fulfilled or because of some difference of opinion.

This way, the very meaning of friendship is changing.

Everyone needs friendship. But we create friendship because of need. But if genuine friendship is formed, that is nice and sweet.

WORKING LIKE THE SUN

We often say time is not in our favour? How can time be in our favour? Do we know the value of time? The tired body needs rest but we go about doing all sorts of things. When it is time for work we go to sleep. Added to this are our irregular food habits and worthless conversations.

One can be healthy if one takes food and rest at right time. Elders say that six to eight hours sleep is adequate and one has to sleep at night and not to wander. But we don't listen. All living beings sleep at night only. It is right to follow the principles of nature.

Going against nature only means we are turning back our body and mind. In earlier days even if one attended a late show or a marriage, the next day used to be a rest day to rejuvenate oneself.

Now it is not possible to do so. Everything is fast–fast life, fast foods. Though our life expectancy has gone up from 48 years to 55 years we should ask ourselves whether we are living with robust health. One should not think that food is the one that tastes good and sleep is the one that induces to close our eyes. At least one should follow proper timings which is a blessing in itself.

The one who measures time alone can be a correct person. A person who works hard can know correct time. He gets tired at appropriate time because he starts work on right time and completes on right time. He has no use for clock. Time becomes his companion. With that power he knows the time.

In fact only a sluggish person needs a clock.

PRACTISE WHAT YOU CAN

We often compare ourselves with others. We argue with ourselves why we do not reach the level of others who seem to achieve much.

In the market we come across several shops doing the same type of business. When there are two vegetable shops side by side, one seems to be doing roaring business where as the other one seems to have no buyers at all. When both of them are selling the same goods why is this difference in success!

We see this kind of difference in other types of business as well. There are many factors behind this difference. It is wrong to say a successful person is more intelligent than a person who is not so successful. If one person is intelligent in a particular thing, another person may be intelligent in some other thing.

It is important for us to know in which we have interest, aptitude and diligence. Then only we can select a work which is suitable to us and we will certainly prosper in that. It will be a mistake to think that since the other person is successful in a particular area. We too can be equally successful.

We should eat food only when we are hungry. If we start eating just because the other person is eating we will fall ill. If we choose a suitable work we can achieve supremacy with ease.

The crocodile is strong in water. Our capabilities are in the area in which we are good.

ANGER OF THE WEAK

Everyone knows that one's anger is one's enemy.

But,don't we get angry? We do get angry. That anger causes pain to our ownselves.

Recently, a friend of mine said-

"I don't know why, but I get angry very often now a days. But it does not last even for a while. When seized with anger I abuse the person in front of me and later repent why I did that. To compensate, I pacify the person and try to do some good for him. Then only I get back my peace. My anger has become the anger of the weak."

I thought that the anger of the weak he is talking about is good because in the process the person who is being abused by him is benefitted.

"One's own peace can be one's own safeguard", but that peace should be psychological rather than physical.

Some, Oh Lord, have long lasting anger. Some others speak softly but hide their anger in their hearts. That anger waits for proper time. Then it affects the person's life like a snake bite.

Since we do not have this type of anger, we should be happy with the anger of the weak. Because of this anger, we lose something ourselves and try to do some benefit to the other person.

So the anger that benefits others is a good anger.

"HE IS A GOOD ONE, POOR FELLOW!"

If anyone does a good deed to us, or helps us in our need we tend to say, "poor fellow".

"He got a job for my son, poor fellow."

"When I faced hardship, he helped me with money, poor fellow."

What is this? Why do we call a person "poor fellow" when he does so much for us? It is indeed a great injustice.

When we say, "Very good person, poor fellow", we are showing him sympathy. Sympathy is for the helpless. A good person is a strong person but not a helpless one.

If any one is very clever, we will praise him saying,"Oh, oh, he is very very clever!".

"Very good person, poor fellow!" "Oh, oh, he is very clever!" Are these the right words to be used?

The phrase "poor fellow" is used only as a mannerism. But this results in bad for doing good.

Now a days, we hardly come across people who help others.

So, let us be grateful to those who help us. Let us do another good deed in return.

It is not right to relegate a good man to a lower category and place a manipulative person on a higher category.

Let us stop referring to a good man as a "poor fellow."

WE SHOULD RECIPROCATE

We all think about our work only. "Please do this for me. Only this one," we request others. "Mine is a very little work. You can get it done easily," we plead. True. But do we ever think that the other person has many obligations like this. We don't understand his discomfort.

"I never asked you for anything till now. Do this for me and I will remember it for ever," we implore. Possible, this is the first demand we made.

The other person may be having many people like us. Each one of them must be asking for only one favour. Can he meet all their requirements? Every one has his own limitations.

We have expectation from our point of view and are not considering his limitations. If he does not oblige us we find fault with him.

Even we get opportunities to do good to others within our limitations. So we should ask ourselves whether we are helping others.

We should never be one sided whatever be the reason. Every one should do what one is capable of doing. We should not have the tendency to say, "What do I get if I come to your place? What will you bring me when you come to my place?"

When we help others we also get help from others when we need it.

DO YOU KNOW ABOUT YOURSELF?

Are we really thinking of ourselves?Are we concerned about our physical and mental well-being? Are we taking enough care of ourselves? Do we know what is good for us?

The answer is definitely in the negative.

We are not giving up the thing which is harmful to us. We are not adopting the one which is good for us. How can anyone be happy and contented with this sort of attitude?

Nothing can be far from the truth than to say that we are only concerned about others and are giving more importance to their well-being.

First-we have to care for ourselves. We should not neglect our ownselves. To start with, we should have care and love for ourselves. Then only,we will be able to love our family. We will be able to set right our family.

If one cannot do even this much, it is hypocrisy to say that one is living for society and working for the betterment of the country.

Slogans like,"The whole world is family" and "world citizens" are very pleasing to the ear.

As a basic thing one should love one's own self.

One should love one's own family. Then only, one could love those around him. It is enough if everyone could do this much. Then the whole world would become a single family.

So, let us think of ourselves first. Let us think of our welfare. Ultimately our welfare is the welfare of the society at large.

UNHURT GOODNESS!

We often say, "We may forget physical hurt but we cannot forget an insult all our life."

Why so? Perhaps the wound caused to the body can heal but not the one that is caused to the heart.

Whose word hurts us? The word that comes from those whom we love and our own people is what hurts us the most. We just don't care for those words which come from an insignificant person.

Indeed it hurts when those whom we love insult us. But they also loved us by words and deeds. How can we forget that? Having got so much love from that person, why should we get hurt if once in a while a harsh word comes? How unjust!

That means we are nullifying that person's love and all the good he has done for us, just because of a small word.

We may say so many things but how much love do we have for others? Now a days, we come across only a few people who genuinely care for us. On the pretext of some harsh word, we are losing a rare person and console ourselves that our self-respect had been offended. We are so irrational as to say, "We may partake goodies but not insults."

There are so many who talk sweetly and exploit us without any return? Are such people good ?

It is only the person who feeds that can hurt us.

It is only the one who loves that can insult us.

WORK WHILE YOU ARE BUSY

One can cope with work only when one is busy. Thinking that it is a small job and it can be done anytime, and also thinking that some other job is a very great job and should be done with a lot of contemplation and leisure, we postpone almost all jobs which never get started.

When things get delayed,we also develop a certain detachment.So much so, many schemes which we initially consider as good ones look useless later on.

That is why it is good to be always busy. We can do more work when we are pressed for time. Just as iron is soft when it is heated, we have control over work under pressure.

All jobs are not worth doing. It is good to do good deeds. But it is more important to leave out bad deeds. It is because bad deeds yield bad results many more times than good deeds do.

There should be a sequence. "Order of priority" helps to complete all works on time. If we do first thing last and the last thing first, it not only does not yield expected results but also enmeshes us in problems. So planning is very important.

If we start doing a thing, we can complete it however big it may be.If we are frightened thinking "Oh, it is a very big job", it results in nothing.

It is a blessing to have many jobs which need to be completed. Only to have leisure and good food is a curse. Hard work is indeed a good fortune.

HABITS CAN DIE

"It is easy to quit smoking.I have done it several times," said an English man. This is what a bad habit is all about.

It looks as if we are quitting. In no time, we yield to the temptation telling ourselves, "It's OK, no problem."

We know that the habit is harming us.We know that giving it up will result in good mental and physical health. We also know that our family members and all those who love us will be happy.

Yet, why are we becoming its slaves? It is because we are in the hold of that addiction for very long.

That habit, while being formed, is very humble. It approaches us gradually. At last it will over power us.

Will the thieves enter our house if we are awake? In the same way if we are alert, no bad habit can reach us.

If you are addicted to something, don't neglect it thinking, "Let me see, I will give it up later." It is today and now that the habit should be ended. For that, we need strong will and determination.

Before we became victims of that habit, we were happy. After giving it up, we will be more happy. The habit that plagued us in between should be buried.

Whatever be this bad habit, let us give it up today saying, "For me, it is dead."

MAJORITY SHOULD AGREE

We enjoy seeing the other person defeated. We feel very comfortable. But we can't digest the success of others. So we invent several meaningless reasons.

We say, "Time favoured him", or "He is lucky." Or we criticise, "What does he know?"

Sometimes we also bet. "Just watch. This does not last long. Very soon we will witness his downfall." We are forgetting something here. We are insulting the people who credited him with success.

One industry is prospering means the product of the same is popular among people. A cinema is successful because the audience liked it. Thus if we criticise a success we should understand that we are insulting people and their opinion.

If we see the history of any winner in this world we see relentless industry and perseverance behind him. History proves that there are no short cuts to success. We should be inspired by the success of other person. For that we should purge ourselves of envy and jealousy.

We always confront some problem or the other. As if that is not enough why do we burden ourselves with additional grief for the success of the other person?

We should rather compete with the capabilities of the other person instead of searching for his weaknesses.

TOO MUCH INTERFERENCE IS FUTILE

Suppose some one seeks our help we go overboard. Even if he asks for a little help we delve deep into the problem and accomplish the task.

So far it is good and the other person is also happy. He may praise us saying "You have done a lot for me. Many, many thanks."

That pleases us no end, we go out of our way to sort out all his problems and bring down our self-respect. They look down on us thinking "Why should he interfere with all our affairs?" and may ultimately say "That is enough."

This is because we never asked ourselves, "Why all this trouble? Where is the need?" This will lead to a situation where those who got benefited from us start disliking us.

Our very visit may embarrass them. They start thinking, "Why has he come now? What a pest!" We come to know of their feelings and are hurt.

We crave for someone else's sympathy complaining, "See this fellow. I did so much for him. But look at the way he behaves towards me."

Why all this trouble! We should be useful to others only to the extent they need us.

When we do good beyond a point that becomes bad. So we should be within our limits not expecting any gratitude for all that we have done. Then only others will have warmth and respect for us.

WHATEVER IS LOST IS LOST

We may say in hundred ways, "What is there in money. It is bad. It corrupts." But no one can deny the importance of money in life. At the same time it is a big mistake to think money is everything in life. No doubt to be stingy is bad. But then extravagance too leads to one's own downfall.

It is all fun and excitement to spend money. We feel great when friends and relatives around us praise us saying, "Aha, he never cares for money."

One feels it is hard to go up crawling but slipping down seems to be easy. We understand how pitiable our condition is when we realise where we have fallen.

No point crying over spilt milk. The same friends and relatives who praised us once will be now heartless to say, "That fellow! For him no stops. He used to spend money like water. However rich one might be, is it the way to spend money? He deserves this plight."

In fact we wasted our own money and did not touch even a paisa of the other guy. No one has continuous steady income. There are ups and downs. So one has to save while one has money.

Just because we have a medical shop we do not use medicines without reason. Similarly we should not spend money wastefully just because we have money. In fact money is a wonder drug that meets all our needs.

CONFLICT

Someone known to us rings up. Or someone else drops in. Then we happen to be busy. We may be moody. We may not talk to them properly. Sometimes we may say something unpleasant.

Later on, we have prolonged worry.

"We might not have replied properly. Perhaps we said some wrong things. I wish I had not said that. Perhaps this was all unnecessary." So thinking, we worry ourselves to death.

If possible, we contact that person again and get some comfort. If there is no such opportunity, we punish ourselves. Is there any reason in punishing ourselves thus?

But now that the word is uttered, what can you do about it? The other person might have thought the way he wanted. It is over. What can we do about it?

Sometimes we ourselves misunderstand even though the other person had not. We don't even think that others are also like us.

What can be done? Everyone has his problems. Is it possible to sit leisurely and peacefully always ? The other person should also understand the same.

If they really love us, they will understand us. If they don't care for us, they will misunderstand us anyway. We need not care for them. We should put an end to those thoughts which rob us of our mental peace and result in a conflict.

SILENCE IS THE WEAPON

Some people look forward to hurt us, to feel happy when we are suffering, to make fun of us when we are defeated. Some others write anonymous letters abusing us and feel satisfied.

There are others who without reason or rhyme treat us as enemies and say hurting words even when we keep quiet. When we try to do some good within our capacity, there are people who search for meanings and interpretations which are contrary to what is intended.

If we pay attention to their words and feel sad, they will be the victors because their aim is to hurt us, make us unhappy and to revel in that.

So, if we don't care for this type of sadists, that will serve as a shock treatment to them.

That silence will be a weapon to break them apart.

There is no one who can be above criticism. There is no way of pleasing everyone.Our conscience is our witness. Our conscience is our judge.

We have to grow in a way to surprise others and not to fall to evoke their pity.

If so, the criticism of pessimists in bad taste will not bother us.We won't hear the voices which ridicule us. We don't observe the games of anonymous people. As long as we don't harm others, no one else can harm us.

DON'T HUMILIATE MOTHER

The moment she hears, "Mother, I am hungry" she leaves aside other things to give food to the person who sought. There are many such good souls in this country. That is why we call this country a sacred land.

Gandhiji said that a hungry person's God is food itself.

There is poverty in our country. There are a number of people deprived of food, clothing and shelter. Yet when a person is hungry and seeks food he is fed by our mother Bharat. We don't remember the teachings of the Buddha, Nagarjuna and Vivekananda and the greatness of Ramayana and Mahabharata.

The fact that we forget our country as the land of action and the best in the world only shows our ignorance.

We abuse ourselves, we fight among ourselves, and we humiliate ourselves. We have abandoned the thought that we are lucky to be born in this country. We always praise foreign countries and never realise the greatness of our country. This is our misfortune.

We have come to the conclusion that Sri Krishna's words in the Gita saying, "Work is yours and the result is mine" are impractical nowadays.

We have orphanages. There are many asylums which are taking care of people. Either consciously or unconsciously we have imbibed respect for elders and the aged. Everyone should be proud to utter, "Jai Bharat".

The publicity about starvation deaths is unfounded. We should not believe it. We should wish to be born again and again in this land.

SMALL IS BEAUTIFUL

We normally don't care for small things. We think that only big things matter.

Recently my niece asked me, "What does L.L.B. mean, uncle?"

"It is a law course, child," I said.

"It is O.K. What is the expansion of L.L.B.?" she asked again. Now I had to scratch my head. I didn't know the answer.

Later on, a friend who had done his doctorate came to me. I asked him the same question. He too had no answer. At last, I came to know what L.L.B. means. That is Legum Baccalaureus (Bachelor of Laws where LL is taken as 'laws').

So, we don't know many things. For example, we don't know the pin code of our address. Even our own house number we try to recall. Some people can't say for sure in what class their children are.

There are people who make elaborate arrangements for marriages. But they don't show enough care for wedding invitations. Sometimes there are many mistakes. These people think that showing off things is important. No wonder even if they forget the most essential marriage thread, **mangalasutram.**

When we can't grasp even small matters, to think that we can understand big matters is just an illusion.

The fact is the great banyan tree emerges from a small seed.

Similarly great deeds are born out of small matters.

Dew Drops 38 Vemuri Balaram

REAL WELFARE

"We are keeping well. Hope you are also keeping well." These are the normal introductory lines of our letters.

This is just a tradition we follow. Actual well being is known only to God.

No one has everlasting difficulties in life.So also, no one can have everlasting comfort and happiness. Even then we think that other persons are happier than us.We think they are very fortunate and have no problems whatsoever. This is where the real mistake is. This comparison is the root cause of our unhappiness.

Whatever be a person's economic standard, he too will have happiness and unhappiness, pleasure and pain, the same way as all of us have.

However, we tend to think that our vicissitude is greater than anyone else's. Then we pray, "Oh, Lord, I would have borne another difficulty better than this. Any pain is agreeable instead of this one. Please God, help me to get over this."

We get over that difficulty. Yet another one appears. Then also we think the same way.

We are also having pleasures in life. But we forget them. We only remember and ruminate over hardships.

Pleasure and pain are natural in everyone's life. Let us not give importance to either of them. Let us have even attitude towards both these aspects.

The taste is not in the thing as such. It is in the tongue. Happiness is not in wealth, but it is within us.

THE FIGURES AFTER ONE ADD TO TO THE VALUE

Children are like gods. There is no doubt about it. But selfish thought starts in the childhood itself. "My doll, my mother, my father" they say hugging us. We like them saying that and behaving that way. We encourage that tendency while bringing them up.

We praise them in their own presence saying, "Our children are very intelligent. They won't part with their things." Even the listeners will appreciate saying, "Oh, how intelligent!"

How the children shape up as adults is not in our hands. At least when they are young it is our responsibility as parents to teach them what is good and what is bad.

It is very important to tell them "You should not eat it alone. You should share it with others. Give your doll to that boy. Let him play for a while. We all should be together." This teaches them equality. The young minds are impressive and they carry lasting impressions.

We all suffer from selfishness. This devil enters us prompting us to do many unjust things and resort to unjust means. It makes us lose the fear of doing wrong. If it is beneficial wrong and unjust things have become acceptable. Thus human being is degenerating. There is no contentment and there is no peace.

Selfishness which is the root cause of all that is evil is a poisonous seed which we are sowing in the young minds. All people accept but only a few can give. All can eat but only a few can feed others.

AT HOME...

We have happiness where we are. But we don't think so and run here and there. We think we will have a break and rest. Having gone there, we become very restless and yearn for getting back home.

Birds and animals all reach their homes after their wanderings. They become part of nature and live freely without a care.

So also every person goes here and there to earn his livelihood.He meets a number of people and does several things. These are all necessary.Then he returns home.

Then there is disgust about routine life. There is an inner struggle to do something different from what one is doing. We search for peace.

We think life is a mechanical circle and aspire for a new place and new comforts...

There is disappointment that we are sleeping and waking up at the same place, doing the same routine work.

But to think that there will be happiness and rest in an alien place which is not congenial and among unknown people is a myth like distant mountains appearing smooth.

It is possible to have happy life within one's means.

Similarly, it is good to seek comfort and happiness at one's own place.

Happiness is there for fish in water, for wild animal in forest and for a person in his own house.

LUCK IS EVERY ONE'S RIGHT

If anyone achieves anything, we immediately list it under"luck".We propagate that he has special opportunities and an invisible supportive hand.

We are not taking into consideration the person's struggle, determination and the sacrifices he has made to achieve what he achieved.

Only laziness waits for luck."It is my fate. Whatever is to happen will happen," is a sort of feebleness which keeps one away from hard work.

When it is time to work hard to achieve results, we search for "luck".

We can be eligible only with self-help.To achieve something, we have to lose something. We should not rationalize that happiness and victory are ours and hardships and defeat are of 'Karma' and fate.

Since luck is God-given, everyone has a right over it and we are all enjoying it. There is no need to make a special effort for luck. If we move forward with hard work, the luck will follow.

Is it possible to have a tree without a seed and a seed without a tree. Similarly will there be a result without an effort? Can we achieve what we want if we just keep waiting for luck?

WE PROMISE NOT TO FORGET

We have many needs. If our need is a genuine one there are many who would like to give a helping hand. But what is happening generally is people accept help and instead of expressing gratitude, they are ready to harm the person from whom they got help.

Because of this even good people are not responding. So people with genuine needs are suffering without help. We have this outward culture to say thanks to every small thing but there is no heart felt gratitude for the person who actually helped us when we were in trouble.

In this short life and in this little world we know we have the responsibility of preserving those people who helped us out of good will.

A person who is successful in preserving these relations can lead a peaceful life with the assurance that there is someone to help when the need arises.

Our life ends without repaying the debt of some. Whereas there are others who don't give us an opportunity even to express our gratitude. One is lucky if one gets an opportunity to repay some one's good deed.

It is said that if a person quenches thirst with water in return we have to give milk to pay back his debt.

If we sign on a promissory note we have no other go except to repay the money. Otherwise the other party sees to it that you repay. We don't need any special training for repaying such debts.

The number of good people will increase when ethics devoid of notices and documents come into vogue.

OUR WORDS ARE NOT OUR WORDS

Do we really have freedom of speech?

Are we able to say freely whatever we have in our mind? Are we able to say what we want to say? No.

We fix our mind in a frame that suits the one before us and yielding to the circumstances, we express our ideas.

Infact our conversation starts with hesitation.

We always talk after much thought, and weighing our words.

Otherwise there will be a lot of misunderstanding. We fear that there will be problems galore if we express whatever we think.

With a view not to hurt anyone, we always shower praise on others and think that is the right way.

What a misfortune not to utter the word which is in our heart! It is so even in the case of wife and children. No exemption anywhere.

This way, perhaps gradually, our individuality and our real self will shrink within us.

Here I am not referring to the right to criticise and to expose political matters. That freedom of speech is not my worry. I am concerned about our own freedom to express what is there in our mind.

Should we be always talking within the frame work of our necessity and the other man's position?

Is this the freedom of speech that we are enjoying?

The real freedom of speech comes only when we can freely, without any hesitation, express our inner thoughts.

WHOSE SHAME?

Whenever we abuse someone, we compare them with animals.We refer to a person as an ass,a dog, and a he-buffalo.

Why should we compare ourselves with animals when we commit mistakes? Do animals commit mistakes as we do? No.

Each animal has a systematic life. It has its own character. There is a method in its life style. They don't change their mind every minute and acquire new addictions everyday.

Then why do we compare people with animals when we want to humiliate them? They don't commit the mistakes committed by the indisciplined people.

Infact, the cattle or the animals do not need a human being for their livelihood. Moreover, human beings are obstacles to their free life. Every human being directly or indirectly is depending on animals.

The animals live as vegetarians or non-vegetarians all their life.We do not know if we are vegetarians or nonvegetarians. We don't have a system in food habits and living style.

We don't have any limit or control. The only great thing about us is that we are able to think.

True! But how far are we able to make good use of our thinking? In what way are we living better than animals?

Who knows, there may be many occasions when animals are ashamed of us and are hanging their heads in shame!

OUR HEALTH

There is no doubt that our health is our wealth. But our health is largely dependent on the nature of our body. Sometimes our thoughts are the root cause of our diseases.

Science gives us a few health principles. True. But over and above, there is a difference from body to body just as our mentality differs from person to person.There are a few things which are either suitable or not suitable to our very selves. If we know these things and follow the rules, we can have perfect health.

There is no logic in saying that the other person enjoys good health in spite of all bad habits and when it comes to us why we can not have the same good health. We should not compare ourselves with others and should not acquire those habits at the cost of our own health. There are so many differences between a person and another person in looks itself. In this unlimited creation, are there things which are similar except a few thoughts?

Disease is different and ill health is different. Some people move about in a healthy way in spite of disease.Some people seem to be suffering from some disease in spite of good health.We should understand that our physical and mental disposition is the root cause of our state of health.

There are many things which are beyond science. The irrational fear of disease causes us more ill health. The body too has a nature like that of mind. It is always good to behave according to the nature of our mind and to live according to the nature of our body.

FOR OUR FELLOW

There are many Telugu Foundations in our state as well as in other states. They give awards to several people every year.

But generally,the awardees are not Telugu people. From some where and from some other language they are selected to be honored. Perhaps they think that Telugu people do not deserve these awards.

Moreover,one cannot hear even one Telugu word in those gatherings. Perhaps it is because the person to be honoured does not know Telugu. Besides, they are proud to proclaim, "I don't know much of Telugu."

This way, they are Telugu Foundations only for name sake. There is nothing Telugu about it. How far can these organisations serve our Telugu culture?

Infact, we don't admire our Telugu people. We don't recognize the greatness of our own man. We tend to be critical and try to find only faults. Then we publicise these findings far and wide to undermine the person and derive a lot of satisfaction.

We don't want our Telugu person. There is no compatibility with a person from our district. If a person from our town comes up, we cannot stand that. If that person happens to be our relative, our agony increases.

So why are we distancing ourselves from our own person? That person may be of some use to us some time. Even if he does not have that inclination to help, we should leave him to his fate.

We should not spoil our time and mind by treating him as an enemy.

WHY DO WE NEED EMPTY WORDS?

Sometimes relatives, friends or acquaintances happen to visit us. Then they may ask "What are you doing?" We tell them about our job. Immediately they say "Is that all? We thought you were in a big job."

Then they start humiliating us by asking "Did you not buy this? Did you not buy that? At our home..." They go on boasting about their high profiled lifestyle.

We keep quiet because we don't want to be rude. That helps them boast more.

They visit us, accept our hospitality and even without mentioning as much as, "Thank you", they search for some lacuna to comment upon. This is nothing but sadism.

Their words hurt us. But we respect relationship and keep everything to ourselves. The life which had been smooth and peaceful till now suddenly becomes incomplete as if lacking something. The visitors go away leaving our family members disturbed.

This is the gift they have left with us. There are some others who find fault with our hospitality as well.

There is nothing wrong in getting rid of such relationship and bonds with least hesitation. The relationships without love only disturb mental peace.

Where there is love, there cannot be ridicule or irony. Those with real warmth alone are our relatives.

ENOUGH TO REMEMBER WHAT YOU ARE

Some people remember people, their names, caste and other details very well. As for us, we hardly remember. When we meet a person we rake our brain to recall where we met him. We don't remember the name. With this the other person gets annoyed.

"How can you remember me? I am too insignificant for you, not worth remembering. You are a great person" is the volley of words filled with sarcasm, irony and ridicule that are directed at us.

We may not be ungrateful or mean to forget people and their goodness. But within the scope of our small brain a few things escape.

Suppose the other person helps us remember we react saying, "Sorry, I couldn't place you immediately. Please don't misunderstand me." We even go to the extent of apologising. But they don't give us that opportunity and continue to hurt us with words.

"What harm did I do to him? Some people have sharp memory and some don't have sharp memory. I belong to the second category. Why can't this man understand? What would he gain by hurting me?" is the trend of our thoughts.

Not that others don't forget. Everyone forgets. It is rare to have intellectual capability to recall everything when woken up from deep sleep. What are we common people before them.

We struggle to remember, try to recall and while we are still in that process the other person comes down on us charged with emotion. What can we do about it? It is unnecessary to get hurt by such misunderstanding and outburst.

WE SHOULD LOOK TOWARDS LIGHT

Love is a unique feeling. Those who have spiritually matured can distribute their love to all. The love that results in attachment to another person is like an addiction.

Those of us who are caught in this snare cannot think of others. Those with true love can look at everyone with equanimity. There is an element of sacrifice in love.

Those of us who are in the mire of attachment mistake it to be love. We don't recognise it as a characteristic of our weak mind. There is selfishness in our attachment. If we don't get in that attachment the satisfaction we imagined we get frustrated.

We are upset if a person with whom we are attached is separated from us even for a while. This kind of attachment we may develop not only towards human beings but even towards money, possessions and other materialistic things and status.

We see many people who carefully plan for their future and old age. The care they take is only about physical aspects. We don't think about spiritual aspects of future.

We think the people we love will be with us till the end. We are pained when they behave contrary to our expectation. Keeping these things in mind we have to develop our mind spiritually even while we are young.

We should not search for a solution only when confronted with a problem.

Not forgetting the basic principle that all physical attachments lead to complexities, let us develop only strong and selfless love within us.

LET THEM LAUGH, WHAT DO I CARE?

We don't think much. We understand far little. Though we know only a human being can think we are lazy to exercise our brain. We do everything on the spur of the moment. We use no discretion or give no thought for propriety before doing or saying anything.

Our selfishness is the driving force. So we yield to it leaving aside finer feelings because for us getting what we want is important.

We tell ourselves that we need not wait for an appropriate time. We don't hesitate even to beg for a favour. We don't care if we are causing trouble for others. We don't mind even if others despise us since our ultimate aim is to get what we want.

In fact we should have hesitation in asking a favour. We should give a thought to the way we are embarrassing others. We think we should aim at getting our work done and nothing else.

But don't we have hesitation or doubts? Of course, we have. We doubt other person's capability. We doubt other person's power. We suspect his greatness.

Because we are so narrow in our thinking that we cannot accept anyone can be greater than us. This kind of cheap mentality hinders our growth and reduces us to the level of begging.

Suppose it is not wrong to ask for something which we don't have, then we should ask ourselves if our mind is broad enough to share our possessions with others.

DARKNESS GIVES BIRTH TO LIGHT

Ever since our childhood we are used to be under the control of someone and be disciplined. At home parents, outside elders and in school teachers restrict, control and direct us. So we don't have independent thinking.

As a result if anyone asks something we are not in a position to answer them. We don't have that much knowledge and understanding.

Leave alone not knowing answers, we don't have courage even to ask questions. Whenever we ask we always go wrong. Sometimes we don't even know how to exchange pleasantries.

If we see a mother carrying a child we ask, "Can't your child walk?" Is it the way to greet a mother and a healthy child?

If we happen to see a person known to us hurrying we wonder what might have happened and ask him the same. With this kind of trivial thinking we lost sight of anything good. Always in doubt we don't know how to talk intelligently. Our talk irritates the person no end.

Anyway we have evolved this way. Atleast we should see that our children are given opportunity to question. When we talk to them we should explain things properly. They should be given independence to ask questions. When they start asking why or what of anything we should explain to them leisurely and scientifically.

With patience and skill we should teach good things to our children. We should allow them to take initiative.

Ordering is the quality of ignorant people. Explaining well is the quality of wise people.

FRIDAY MONEY

We have a few sentiments. As long as they do not harm others and do not cause any inconvenience, there is no problem.

There is a sentiment which stops us from giving money to others on Friday.We fear that all our wealth will go to the other person. Is there any propriety in saying, "Today is Friday, so it is not done."

We may not give away the money free. We may stop charities on that day. There is nothing wrong in that. But how horrible it is to have Friday sentiment when it comes to repaying a loan or paying wages!

Then we should not accept any money on Friday. We should not ask others to work for us. We should not buy anything on that day.

No.We don't do that. We think that it is very good to accept money on Friday and to buy new things to be kept at home even if it means borrowing.

One earns money only when one works hard. It could be physical labour or intellectual work. Will it affect you if you pay wages on Friday for hard work rendered?

We should be able to help others and be able to meet their needs. The sentiment regarding Friday is not essential.

Will the Goddess of wealth make her presence felt only on Friday?

Goddess of wealth will permanently reside in the house of an industrious person.

THE BEGINNING OF THE END IS NOW

Will our children look after us in old age? May be they will not. So we are worried from now onwards. Because of this worry, we are separating our children from now onwards.

If there are two children, one child is pampered by mother and another by father."My son will certainly look after me," says mother."My daughter will care for me," says father.Thus father and mother are dividing the children.

Children are becoming stubborn and diverting from the right path because of their parent's love.

This is the mistake of the parents.

Thinking of the old age, the ill health that would trouble the old age, that helplessness, dependency to which children may not respond favourably...

All these are meaningless thoughts.

Thinking of some unknown future, we are getting attached to one particular child and are dividing our own children.

Whether the children will look after us or not is to be left to later times. First, let us concentrate on their future and love all our children equally.

Our goodness and our good deeds will stand by us in future.

They will protect us from dependency.

BEFORE CHARITY BEGINS

We do not get into a rickshaw without bargaining. We don't buy vegetables without finding out the rate. We give alms only after ensuring that the other person is physically challenged.

So we love money.Since human existence is difficult without money, we take so much care. Will all the rich show charity? No.

But there are a few charitable persons among us who give thousands and lakhs in charity. Normally those who give such large charities are businessmen, or artistes.

These people give out their hard-earned money in charity to educational institutions,temples,hostels etc., The charity aimed at the welfare of the society is a great one.

There is no doubt about it.

There are a few who are employed with these charitable people. They stay with these people all their lives. They trust the person with whom they are working.

So it is essential that the charitable people look after the interests of those who are working with them.

They should give them suitable remuneration and see that their families do not face any financial hardships.

There are some great people who look after their staff as if they were their own children and also give huge charities. I wish every charitable person belonged to this category.

ATTRIBUTING ATTACHMENT TO CHILDREN!

At every pilgrim centre and at every sacred place we visit, we offer the hair of our children. If children cry saying, "I won't give my hair", we threaten them saying, "Don't talk like that. Apologise, otherwise God will be angry."

We offer hair to indicate that we should not have any attachment. Then what is it that we want our children to be detached from for which we compel them to give their hair? Will God bless only when this is done? Will our children be happy ?

The other person is in a hurry and shaves the children's head with superfast speed. It hurts and the children start crying. We don't bother much about it. Besides, we insist on children's fasting before visiting God. We console them saying, "Don't cry, my child. That is wrong. You will have refreshments and milk after seeing God." What does all this mean?

Is it necessary to starve before seeing God?

After all the rituals, we come home. The children are teased by their friends and classmates.

We do not understand how much agony the children undergo till the hair grows. We don't recognise their pain. Is punishing God-like children the way to protect them?

WE HAVE TO STOP SOMEWHERE

Everyone has a brain. There is some intelligence and some ignorance. Some people remain ordinary whereas some others are recognised as intellectuals. However great an intellectual may be, even he has his limitations. He can think of anything within these limitations.

It is a mistake to think that a person who is great in a field should be great in every field. Some people are egoistic to think they are knowledgeable and can discuss any subject because they have several degrees and have written several books.

It is better for a person to grow in a field where he has made a name instead of thinking he is number one everywhere. It is enough for a doctor to diagnose a disease. He can become a great doctor.

If one has a good sense of observation he can become a writer. If a director has creativity he can become a great director.But there is no guarantee that a great writer can be a great director.

It is essential for a boatman to know how to swim. Because when the boat sinks swimming alone can save him. Other skills don't help him at that time.

We should know what our strengths are and we should realise what our weaknesses are. Then only we can see our intellectual limitations clearly. A person who goes ahead with the knowledge of his limitations and scope will have a successful life.

HAVE NO PREJUDICE

Everywhere one comes across cheating. Everywhere one comes across deceit and lies. We are not able to know what is truth. Though there are some good and noble people we tend to suspect them also because a large percentage of people do not keep their word.

By nature we are not angry people. Yet we cannot witness the wrong doings. Even if we see we can do nothing about them. We do not resist and fight. We are not heroes. We are just common people.

We are helpless before hardships we encounter outside. So when we come home we give vent to our anger and frustration. We know we are falsely accusing our own people. Yet that is our helplessness.

Everyone is deciding beforehand that the other person is a bad person. Because of this everyone is trying to be smarter than the other person by scheming and deceiving. At the end both are in trouble and no one is benefited.

This leads to restlessness. No one seems to be happy. Everyone pretends to be happy outwardly but in fact no one is happy. All people know what is good and what is bad. Yet they have a false belief that good has no place in this world. They are under the illusion that it is safe to be bad.

It is sheer madness to think that there is good outcome for bad. How can a good thing result in bad? The day we consider the other person to be like us we get solutions to all our problems. We all can live together happily.

IS IT BETTER TO HAVE MORE KNOWLEDGE?

We fill our stomach with all sorts of things even when we are not hungry. In the same way, we fill our mind with all sorts of thoughts.We think about every thing.There is conflict over everything. We don't even consider whether it is necessary or not and continue to think and upset ourselves in the process.

What are our problems? What are our necessities? How to solve these problems? We should only think this much and put those thoughts into action. Then we will get good results. No, we do not stop there.

Many unnecessary thoughts plague us. We go for unnecessary knowledge. Why? Is there any necessity to possess this knowledge? Isn't it enough to have sufficient knowledge?

Infact, we don't allow our mind to be at peace. We think of unnecessary things and imagine them to be big problems. Then we lead over burdened lives.

The weight of our thoughts is more than our physical weight. Why do we carry this extra luggage?

Instead of indulging in unnecessary thoughts, we should think of ourselves. We should understand ourselves.

Just as unlimited desires disturb mental peace, so also useless thoughts torment us. It is necessary to put a full stop to these thoughts in the interest of our physical and mental health.

ONCE THE NEED IS MET...

We have all sorts of superstitions. If we wear a particular dress, we are sure to be successful. If we travel by a particular train, we can complete our work without a snag. So we have a good number of sentiments. And we never give them up.

But do we have the same attachment with people especially with those who helped us? "That person helped me on that day and I got benefitted because of that person. So I should always remember him. Even if I cannot return what he has done to me, at least it is my duty to express my gratitude." But do we really feel this way? Difficult to say.

We use sentiments only for selfish purposes.

It is said that if a person quenches our thirst with water,we can repay his debt by giving him milk when he needs.

But we express our gratitude only at the time we receive the needed help. "You came to me like God and helped me. I can never forget this," we tend to say holding his hands.

Later on, we avoid him. Then we forget about it.

Forgetfulness is a great boon to human beings. That is why we are able to forget the difficulties we have undergone in the past. We live with hope about future. It is all very good but to forget the one who helped us is indeed a curse.

FEROCIOUSNESS IS NOT RIGHTEOUSNESS

Some times we lose balance because of certain circumstances. That results in mistakes in work and harshness in words. Then even wrong looks right.

We think what all we have done is correct. Later on if we think calmly we realise how hasty those decisions were. By the time we realise it may be too late to correct them.

When we say harsh words in a moment of emotion we lose good deeds as well as good people for ever. If anyone points out our mistakes we should think calmly how much truth is in it. It is wrong to think that none should find fault with us or oppose us. The egoistic feeling that only ordering about is our duty is self-detrimental.

It is not a great thing to challenge everyone for everything. Propriety and impropriety should guide our behaviour. We should take right decisions at right time. We need some time for that.

When we strike a ball against a wall with force it will come back with equal force to strike our face. We alone are responsible for this and no one else.

Instead of doing things without due consideration and regretting it later it is better not to do at all. We should not develop this attitude of doing wrong things first and regretting later.

Whatever work we do, whatever words we utter they should be righteous. Our words and deeds should make others regret and should not cause any regret to ourselves.

WHATEVER LITTLE YOU GIVE IS GREAT FOR HIM

No one wants to live on someone else's charity. From early morning till night one wants to be engaged in one's own work to stand firmly on one's own feet.

It is not agreeable to us to go around pleasing everybody for selfish gain or to walk with a staff as support to gain others sympathy.

However independent our thoughts may be, under certain circumstances we may have to seek others help.

There is nothing wrong in seeking help so much as we require. But when we get an opportunity we have to pay back the same even if it means we have to do manual work. Similarly others who need our help approach us.

We get enormous happiness in helping others within our capabilities. In this social life helping each other is inevitable and it is not wrong.

Sometimes we think it would be nice if our work is done without much problem. If there is no risk and everything is gain our happiness knows no bounds.

But the truth is the gain that comes without any effort or sacrifice does not make us happy. The gains we get freely will last only for a while. But the result we get out of our hard work always remains with us and gives us comfort and happiness.

We show great skill in receiving things from others. Similarly we should have this great quality of looking forward to help our fellow beings whenever and wherever possible.

NO POINT IN CURSING

We don't read literature,yet we are literary scholars. We don't patronise arts, yet we are artists. We can never be impartial, yet we are good critics.

We cry hoarse saying, "Literature is soiled. It has gone to dogs", but we don't support literary magazines. We lecture about the need for good literature. We organise seminars.If necessary we engineer literary movements. But we never encourage a literary magazine.We never buy a magazine for reading. This is how we patronise arts. Each one reads one's own writings. There is no need to read the writings of others. But we are capable of criticising even without reading.

As for cinemas, we abuse every movie, "They have double meaning dialogues, sexy dances, unbearable crime. Infact no one can view these movies with families,"is our ceaseless criticism.But we don't support even one single artistic film. We appreciate award winning movies but don't support them.

The same is the case with magazines. We don't read any magazine. But we criticise everyone of them. "What sort of stories full of crime and sex! Oh, these journals are really spoiling the readers. In the name of literature they run big business." We conduct meetings in this regard but there is no one to analyse a magazine and say what is wrong with that.

People in large numbers can get the governments they need. A great number of audience alone can give patronage to good films. A large number of readers alone can judge the magazines.

FRIGHTENING THOUGHTS

Many fears chase us all our life.

We are afraid to sleep alone. We are afraid to travel alone. We are afraid that some serious disease may kill us. Thus, unnecessary fears continue to trouble us.

But these fears are not really dangerous. They don't kill us. Even then,we try to escape them instead of getting out of that fear. We are afraid even to be freed from that fear.

Why should we yield to these fears? Why can't we face them? We know that it will not harm us, yet we adjust thinking, "What if I am afraid? What do I lose?"

Thus we yield to this phobia and try to escape from that. Then we acquire one more fear. Again we compromise. If we go on compromising like this, our life will be filled with phobias.

We have enough strength to face difficulties. But the very thought that there will be a difficulty is troubling us.

Instead, one should be determined to gain control over that fear. If we work decidedly in this direction, the fear will be vanquished.

As a result, we can live a life free from all phobias and hesitations.

LIGHT IS THE ONLY ANSWER TO DARKNESS

We travel by bus, train or aeroplane.

Not knowing when the bus will arrive, on which platform the train arrives and through which gate one has to board the plane we get confused first and then become panicky.

We enquire from the employees there.They get irritated not understanding why these passengers are so panicky because that employee has full information and command over travel timings. Those people who know everything tend to look on us as ignorant people.

What to do? We are also capable people in some other area. But in an area in which we have no knowledge we are naturally at lower rung. It is no reason that those people should not humiliate us.

Though they do their duty everyday they should not be negligent towards it on any day. We breathe in air every second. That gives us life. The work we do every day gives us our livelihood.

It is not civilised behaviour to take the other person lightly or to talk contemptuously. It is their duty to treat every person as a special person. If they cannot do they should better leave the job.

The house where we live looks ever green to us. We are not disgusted with the food we eat. We have sumptuous meals three times a day.We are also not irritated with sleep which we get every day.

Rather we look forward to an opportunity to go to sleep. This ever fresh feeling should be there in discharging our duty as well. Then only one can be responsible citizen and can be of use to society.

TRUTH IS LIFE TO THE WORD

We may talk of high things. We may impress others by exhibiting our skill in communication. We may leave others stunned with our logic. We may win their appreciation with good language and diction.

One can even bury truth and create a wonderful new story with imagination. But when the strong winds of truth blow all these wild imaginations will collapse like a pack of cards.

Just because one murderer is proved to be innocent, an innocent man cannot become a murderer. The pleasure that we were able to make the other person speechless by weaving our own magic of words will not last long.

That skill should be shown in doing good to others. One should not resort to evil by talking in a clever way. Empty promises and words just vanish into the thin air. They will never touch the hearts.

Mere argument only exhibit foolishness and lead to nothing. One word of truth is enough to wipe out all arguments. That is the power of truth.

We clean our mouth, our face. We brush our teeth and clean our tongue. Here we are only removing dirt but not intending our tongue to be clear. We don't get good words just because we scrap and clean the tongue.

We forget that all troubles and conflicts are due to wagging tongue.

Tongue has a remote control in heart. Since the heart is our own to keep the heart pure is in our own hands .

YOU THE UNCONCERNED

I am responsible for environmental pollution. I felled trees. I constructed buildings. I am responsible for not keeping my street clean. I dumped all the garbage from my home on the street.

I am responsible for my children not respecting me. I did not respect my parents. I am responsible for my wife telling lies. I always tell her lies. I am responsible for no one heeding my word in office. I never do what my boss wants me to do.

I am responsible for not having any friends. I don't allow anyone to come near me. I am responsible for my relatives not loving me. I don't love anyone. I am responsible for no neighbour responding to my call. I don't do any good to anyone.

I am responsible for my family members not loving me. I have only self interests. I am responsible for no one sharing my grief. I had not shown any sympathy to anyone.

I am responsible for not being successful. I never worked hard. I am responsible for not having riches. I always chose evil. I am responsible for not having mental peace. I envied others. I am responsible for not having tranquillity. I instigated people to fight.

I am responsible for my poor appetite. I snatched away the other fellow's food. I am responsible for my diseases. I overindulge myself in eating and drinking. I am responsible for every incident, every act and every consequence in my life.

THE PEASANT IS POOR BUT THE LAND IS RICH

It is true that every human being needs food, clothing and shelter. Over and above everyone seeks freedom. Even animals and birds are unhappy if they lose their freedom. That is why a parrot though in a golden cage cannot be happy even for a single moment. The bird that takes wing early morning in search of food has unlimited happiness.

We fought with the British over hundred years and won our freedom. In that struggle thousands of people sacrificied their lives. Today we are enjoying freedom and independence as fruits of their sacrifice. It always happens that one sacrifices and another gets benefits.

The person who sacrifices has no selfish motive that he should enjoy the fruit. There is no guarantee that a person who plants a tree rests under it one day. Yet he plants the tree.

We are born of earth and become one with earth. That is why unconsciously we love earth. There is no fragrance better than that of earth. Every person who does not particularly hate his motherland would like to die there irrespective of number of countries he visited.

We have seen many great people, many rulers, many officers and people of status who would like to reach their place of birth for their last journey. That is the real greatness.

Even though there is hunger and there is poverty our motherland Bharat is not ruled by dictators. We should be born again and again in this land of action. Hail Independent India!

FEEDING ON THE BRAIN

The other sunday I attended a Guruji's meeting. Guruji's disciples took away watches from everyone and said they would be returned at the time of leaving. Guruji said, "Among you there may be doctors, business men and people of high position. But here no one is high or low."

Anyway we were all squatting on the floor forgetting all differences. Why this reminder now?

Guruji continued. "An ignorant person is a burden to the earth. The ones who made fun of me at one point are calling me "diamond" now after my enlightenment and are proud of my company. Is it true?"

One of the audience answered, "Yes, it is true." "Why?" Guruji asked. "Because you say great things" was the reply. Then Guruji said, "May be I am not a great person as an individual, how do you know? You don't know.

"I can observe myself. May my soul be my witness I am not an enlightened person. That means soul is great."

"The nose is like a lock to the brain. It always seeks fragrance. We have to control it," he said as he himself was seated on a chair decked with fragrant flowers. "None of you should move," he ordered like a dictator and continued his speech.

No intellectual, no enlightened would speak for over an hour. While listening to Gurus we should not be conscious of time. On the contrary here watches are taken away and the speech continued for over three hours. This is a virtual punishment.

These people who always insist on limited food, limited talk and self-knowledge do not know about themselves. If a teacher is ignorant his disciple too loses his senses. So it is better to maintain distance from such teachers.

ARE WE NOT AT FAULT?

We don't trust anybody. No one is trusting us. We consider each other to be at fault.

We say, "Now a days no one can trust anybody. Everything is cheating, fraud and lies." Everyone is feeling the same way. When some of us meet, we all feel the same way as if only we were good and the rest of the world was bad.

We think that the society is rotten, there is no value for human beings and everyone is out to exploit us. But are we not part of the society? Are we good people? Are we truthful? Is ours good behaviour?

It is wrong to blame others without reforming ourselves? It is unjust to expect the world to change without first changing ourselves?

We have to trust fellow human beings. We have to love them. Then they will also trust us and love us.

It we start mistrusting everyone, ultimately there will be no one left and we may distrust our own selves.

What is the good we have done to the society? What is the good we have achieved?We should introspect. It is no use blaming the society and considering everyone as a bad person. The good and trust we expect from others should begin from us. We should be eye-witnesses to this.

HERE AND NOW

Everything should be done at the appropriate time.One should enjoy when one is young and should not think that life can be enjoyed after retirement. Then one may not have good health to eat what one wants. There may not be anyone around to listen to what he says.

As students, we can concentrate on studies aiming at good marks and missing the company of friends and enjoyment of childhood.

In the youth ,we have a target. We rush to achieve that and forgo the pleasures of youth.

Our youth is passed without any enjoyment with wife and children and we are not even conscious that we are missing the sweetness of living.

We are forgetting pleasures of today and live in tomorrow. The next day will also pass the same way. We are not living in the present.We are losing comforts and accepting only difficulties. Unknowingly we are asking for such circumstances and regretting in old age for not spending our youth meaningfully.

Just as seasonal fruits are good for health, happiness lies in doing things which are to be done in a particular age.

On the contrary, youthful acts in old age and old age acts in youth become meaningless and unbearable.

LAUGHTER SHOULD BE CENTRED

We like some and we do not like some others. If we say we like everyone that is far from truth. If it is so it is clear that we do not like anyone in particular. That means we just talk to everyone pleasantly and try to become popular.

No one is close to our heart. We spend our time by superficial words and actions.

It is impossible to please everyone. If there is any such person he is certainly a worthless person. Because when we do good to a person without our knowledge we become bad to another.

The person who gets benefited from us also moves away once his work is done. He brags about individuality and goes out of his way to talk about our weaknesses.

It is said that we may not do good to everyone but atleast we should not do bad to a person who did some good for us. A person with sweet words and a bitter mind should never be trusted.

Apart from individuals we also have other likes and dislikes. We develop certain tastes and like a few arts. Then also we cannot be acceptable to everyone.

We can't make lists of right things and wrong things. We cannot divide people into high or low. Every deed speaks of its good or bad.

When there is heart, there is also response. The response is of emotion and love. If a person has these qualities, he is indeed a man with a good heart.

FIND A TIMELY SOLUTION

Friendship with some, bonding with some and relationship with some are inevitable in our lives. We continue to exist with these human relations. But are they permanent bonds? The answer is "no". Yet they are very fragile. A little strain and they snap in no time.

Even if a friend says mockingly, "Get lost. What do you know?" we feel insulted. The friend who has been close to us all this while is distanced in no time. Since we have not learnt how to forgive we suffer from a weak mind which cannot tolerate even a single harsh word.

It is same with the relatives as well. If they don't respond to our invitation once we sever our long standing relationship. Earlier they would have accepted our invitations many a time. But this time they might not have made it for some reason. We do not understand that. All we think is they humiliated us.

If we want to maintain these relations we should develop frankness in our dealings. If we talk over matters the differences will vanish.

Otherwise the words and deeds that hurt us will remain within us growing to gigantic proportions engulfing our character itself. Then we perceive in this world only enemies and wicked people.

Any student who reads his lesson the day he learns becomes the best student. Any person who resolves his problem the day it confronts becomes a great person.

MIND YOUR OWN BUSINESS

Once a person went to an eye surgeon and narrated his trouble. "I can't see any one prospering. I get a burning sensation in my eyes. Please give me some medicine, doctor." The doctor replied, "For a disease like this there is no medicine anywhere."

So there is no need to have burning eyes or stomach. Everyone lives a life of his own, the way he wants it.

Some people think there is happiness in hard work. Some others think life is for enjoyment, for moving with friends, having parties, seeing movies and going for picnics. They take time lightly and waste it.

If they live that way without causing trouble to anyone there is no problem. But it is not so. They go on criticising those who work relentlessly for reaching a goal.

They ridicule as well as sympathise saying, "Poor fellow, he does not know how to enjoy life. He is a workholic. He is unable to enjoy swim in the ocean of happiness which is here in this world."

But these people know in their heart of hearts that they cannot concentrate on any work. So they roam aimlessly bluffing everyone. But they bury this truth within themselves, muffle their conscience and live under an illusion that their method is the right one.

Whatever it is each one's life is his own. One can choose whatever appeals to oneself. The problem is the inability to appreciate other person's work. This is a disease without a cure.

LIFE OF DESIRES

We are middle class people, easily pleased. If we get a cinema ticket on the first day, we are quite pleased. If we get a berth while travelling by train, we are quite happy. When we make a purchase of clothes worth five hundred rupees and get a carry bag free, our happiness is unbound.

We are afraid to think that others, however great they may be, are human beings like us."Oh,that greatness, and that status is only for them! What are we", is our shallow thought.We never think that power is with everyone, greatness and status are everybody's right and we are also eligible. We are satisfied with what we have and don't want anything beyond.

Our ultimate goals are little desires and little pleasures. We draw our boundaries there.

We can never think that we are capable and can achieve a lot, we are brilliant and can be great. Even if a thought crosses to that effect, we chide ourselves saying, "Leave it."

We think it is bad to have desires and life means stifling desires. We would not understand that life is meant for enjoyment and not for ending desires.

This kind of middle class mentality is restricting us. If we fall on the ground we are rewarded only with dust. Suppose we try to catch stars, perhaps we may get stardust.

There should be desires in life.

Our life is meant for fulfilling them.

LOVE CAN BE A PUNISHMENT

What happens when one is in love?Mind is punished. Yes. It may be surprising but it is true.

The other people may not be good enough to receive our love and cause us grief. We think that love should have no boundaries but the love within limits is sacred and lasting.

Love between lovers, parents, sisters, brothers, husband and wife, children, friends...anyone for that matter, if love is not in control it leads to disaster. This is true.

Seeing a couple, we think that they are an ideal couple. Seeing two friends, we think they are born for each other. But love between them is not the same. There is a difference. Oneside can out-weigh the other.

Under a crazy spell,we follow them for love. They develop a contempt for us. They become overbearing and start dominating us. That hurts us. Still we tolerate them because of our love. Sensing this, they weaken us further and derive a lot of happiness.

They think that we love them because we can't help it and cannot live without them.

So be careful. Let us try to control our love. Then only the other person can be in his own limits. Love should always be in limits.That is the real love.

TIME AND MONEY

We don't think much about spending money or spending time. As a result we make our life a meaningless one. No doubt entertainment is essential but can we have entertainment itself as life. Can we bring back time? Can we regain the rupee that has slipped out of our hand?

How much should we allocate to what? Which should be enjoyed to what extent? This discretion is needed for maintaining balance in life.

We should not resort to any entertainment that wastes our time as well as money. Then only we can perform our duty.

If we spend time for reading a good book we can gain some knowledge. Similarly if we listen to good music we gain happiness and health. This way there are a few things which are purposeful. Every rupee we spend should be useful either to us or to others.

J.Krishnamurthy's philosophy, Vivekananda's teachings, Gandhiji's sayings, Paramhamsa's biography, Ramana's words–if we spend time in understanding things related to such great people we should think time itself will be happily thrilled.

Time spent properly is money earned. If it is wasted it results in loss. Both time and money which are two sides of the coin of life are equally important. If we keep this in mind not only we help ourselves but we can also help others.

We should realise that wrist watch is not a decorative piece and money in the pocket is not a burden.

YOU ARE YOUR OWN COMPANION

Whatever we get in life is an opportunity. We should make use of every opportunity.

There is no point in wishing to be in company when one has to be alone and wishing to be alone when one has to be in company.

To be alone is an opportunity. Then there are a few tasks which can be completed. When we have done them we feel happy that we could use our time well when we were alone. When there is work to be done in a team we should make use of that opportunity and conduct ourselves suitably.

When we accept things happily and make proper use of time we see novelty in every day. When we forget the present and look forward to the next day we are losing today's happiness. When tomorrow comes we start thinking about another tomorrow thus ruining our tomorrow.

When we know we came into this world alone and will be leaving it alone there is no point in being depressed, as though missing something and worrying ourselves meaninglessly.

We are alone even when we are amidst many. Even when we are alone there are several people around us. We have to have equanimity of mind. We shouldn't yield to dissatisfaction or lack of courage.

Within our limits whatever comes to us is for our happiness and comfort. We have our share of joy in that. For good taste food is not important, appetite is essential. For comfortable life money is not important, contentment is required.

DON'T OBSTRUCT, TRY TO PROTECT

We are masters of one art or the other. It may be education, music, dance or business. This way everything is an art. Everything needs talent.

It is our duty to pass on whatever we learnt to our children. We have to start teaching them early so that they can practise while we are alive. But we don't do that.

We fear that they may not be able to perform well. They commit mistakes which result in losses.

But we are forgetting the basic thing. While we are alive we will be able to explain their mistakes. We can tell them with examples what caused losses and what helped us to succeed. The children can never learn to be independent if we refuse to handover responsibilities to them.

A day will come when we have to leave everything. Then these people have to shoulder responsibilities. The day we realise this and behave accordingly our children can handle things as well as we can.

Besides they can grow with their independent views on the foundations of our experience. Otherwise we will be responsible for not allowing them to grow like small plants under the shade of a big tree.

There is greatness in giving importance to students. Then they can excel their own teachers.

Similarly children too can excel their parents.

VICTORY IS MINE DEFEAT IS HIS

If anyone achieves something,we say, "Is all this made possible by only one person? All of us worked together for his success. So, he has become great today."

We also question, "Could he have achieved this without us?" If the same person fails, we sneer,"This is his own doing. He never listened to us. Are we responsible for his downfall? As he sowed, so he reaped."

No one wants to have a downfall. No one will be instrumental in bringing about his own ruin.If victory is his, so should be defeat.

When we can say we are responsible for his victory, we must be able to avert his defeat and lead him towards victory. But we don't do that. The reason is we don't have any role in his victory. We cannot accept other person's greatness because of our ego. That is why we criticise in that fashion.

If a person is in a high position, we own him saying, "He is very closely related to me," or " He is my childhood friend. We were very close."

If anyone has fallen from heights,we will say, "I don't know him at all." We don't even talk to him when we come face to face. That means, we own the other person's victory but leave the defeat to himself.

We should realise that it is our duty to wipe away his tears in the same way as we partake of his victory.

LIES SHOULD HAVE PURPOSE

It has become a part of our life to tell lies whether there is a need or not.

True, it is not the time of Satya Harischandra when one tells only truth and nothing but truth. But there is no need to totally give up truth.

When anyone says, "How are you?" We invariably answer, "I am fine" even if things were not all right with us. When someone asks,"How is your business?" we start narrating our woes eventhough our business is running well.

We know it is wrong to tell lies. But can we say whatever is in our mind? Will any purpose be served thus? None. Moreover, there will be troubles. Even when we speak fiery truth, the other one may not be able to withstand that. This kind of extremism is not desirable either for us or for the other person.

Swearing in one's name is a great thing for us. Still we tend to tell lies. In courts, people swear in the name of God and holy scripture to tell the truth but generally they speak untruth.

When others are suspecting us and our conscience is rebuking us, leading a life of lies is not justified in any way.

PRIORITY IS IMPORTANT

We have several tasks to do. But their priority keeps changing. At a particular stage we start an important work. We want to complete it.

Since it is of top priority we dedicate ourselves to it. After a while we happen to start yet another work. We do that and after sometime we pay attention to a new important task. With this priority of previous tasks changes.

Many people do not understand these changes. They criticise us for being busy. Without realising our work pressure they express their anger that we are not caring for them.

"He has become arrogant. Does not care. He is not concerned about us. Earlier he used to do this with full involvement. Now he discards it because he is of higher level," they critise.

They are not able to understand the underlying principle. Just as we start from LKG, UKG and from there to school, college and university even in life one has to grow. Even in shouldering responsibilities one may start light but gradually bigger responsibilities are to be shouldered.

It is a natural process of development to shoulder heavier responsibilities. The discretion to give what importance to what task, how much time for what is very important.

A person with this knowledge becomes great in life. He can shine anywhere. He can enrich anything.

Only such people can be winners.

WORDS SHOULD TOUCH HEARTS

We have many problems in life. We are surrounded by problems at home, with neighbours and even in the street. In addition to this we get entangled in unnecessary problems. One such problem is attending meetings and listening to speeches. In fact these speeches should inspire us. They should be useful by teaching new things and enlightening. There are many such great speeches which stand out in history.

But today we are scared of attending meetings. We may faint with fatigue while listening to their aimless ramblings. Those who are on the dais are least bothered about the audience. They are not pondering even for a moment whether what they are saying is relevant or not.

They tend to speak ceaselessly whatever they like and whatever comes to their mind.

Those who make thundering speeches perhaps think, while the audience are ignorant they themselves are very great and are revealing things which no one else knew. They don't realise that they themselves are ignorant.

The essence of their speech is to talk about their own greatness and undermine others.

Moreover these people do not have time sense. Even if a person speaks meaninglessly for fifteen minutes each one of the audience loses that much time. That way one thousand people together must be losing several hours. A person who takes away so many hours of others time needs to be punished. This talkativeness should also be added to the list of social evils in order to save people.

WELL PROVIDED YET DEPRIVED

We have many parts in our body. We don't use all of them to the maximum. We think only a few parts are essential and make use of them for our work. Let us take for example five organs of senses–eye, nose, ear, tongue and skin. The eye should be used to see the world with equanimity. But we adopt distorted vision that cannot tolerate prosperity of others which causes burning sensation in the eyes.

The nose is for breathing that gives life's energy. On such important nose we tend to carry anger.

When we hear good words we feel happy. When we listen to good music we even forget this world. Such a good ear is lent to others to get ruined.

The skin is like an armour that protects all parts of the body. The skin reacts to every great act. It gets thrilled and tingled. We feel lazy even to clean that skin which is endowed with such great qualities.

As far as the tongue is concerned, its greatness depends on how a person uses it. It shapes every thought into words. It is instrumental in distributing our love, affection and tender feelings. Such a tongue with so many great qualities is used for tongue-lashing others without rhyme or reason. We use our tongue as a weapon for praising self and accusing others.

Since these five sense organs are also knowledge giving organs one should not lead a listless life. A person can live his life to the full only when he energises his latent powers and makes use of them positively.

CONSCIENCE IS A FATHOMLESS OCEAN

We think we can understand others with ease though we cannot understand our own selves. A human being is not a thing to be understood just by speaking or by glancing for a moment.

Even to assess durability and quality of things one needs education and experience in that particular area. But men are different from each other.

Just as all that we see is not real and all that we hear is not true, we cannot determine a person's views and attitudes just by talking to him for a while.

By looking at one's height, weight and form we may judge a person's outward appearance but we cannot come to a conclusion about a person's inner self. Even in defining and judging beauty one differs from the other.

When we cannot have a single opinion about a thing which is obvious and visible it is ignorance to think that we can understand invisible mind and attitude. Usually we tend to be short sighted and narrow minded.

We are always ready to find fault and criticise others. By thinking whatever facet we view to be the real person and by determining his attitude by a single act is like a blind man mistaking a part of elephant itself to be the whole elephant.

We have to study ourselves life long in order to understand ourselves a bit. If that is the state of affairs who are we to decide about others. Time and context cause a particular type of behaviour. That does not reflect the whole person. Those who can easily blame others do not know how to appreciate others.

Bad attitude tends to lookout at others. Good attitude looks into one's own self.

ONE SHOULD BE SENSITIVE

"My mind is very sensitive. I can't stand even the slightest pain. I can't bear anyone hurting me. I am very sensitive." This is how we describe ourselves and feel great about it.

It is good to be sensitive and to support someone in trouble, to be disturbed by an accident and to sympathize with helpless people.

But we interpret sensitivity in some other way. We feel hurt when someone says an unpleasant thing. If we can't achieve what we want, we feel bad. We call this as sensitivity. But this is our selfishness.

I don't mean to say that looking for one's own benefit is bad. But we announce,"I am sensitive." We also think that only we are sensitive and others are not.

We feel a great deal as far as our affairs are concerned. When it comes to others, we are little concerned. This is not sensitivity. We are calling our narrow-mindedness as sensitivity. When anything comes to us easily, we are happy. When we face some difficulty, we become sensitive.

For anybody, one has to react the same way. That is sensitivity. That is "butter-like heart."

THEY ALSO BELONG TO US

"What sin he committed in his previous life, no one knows. He is born blind," is the way we express our sympathy to a blind man. Similarly, when we see lame people we say, "What a fate, he is devoid of two legs." But those people never expect our sympathy. They want our support. Our desperate words make them more helpless.

When we see a leprosy patient, we keep him off saying, "This is the curse of God. Poor fellow is bearing it."

Blindness is not the result of "sin of previous life." One is not "fated" to be lame. Leprosy is not "a curse of God." There was a time when it was not possible to cure leprosy. That is why they created several fears and misapprehensions to keep them out.

But now, leprosy can be easily cured. Still we are victims of ignorance, fear and misunderstanding. These needed to be removed. Leprosy is like any other skin disease. There is a cure for this. One need not hide and suffer.

We are so open in declaring, "I have B.P., no salt please", "I have diabeties. Please don't add sugar to my coffee." Similary, our people should come forward to say,"I have leprosy, I can't take hot coffee."We must be in a position to welcome a leprosy patient when he visits us,"Please come and be seated."

For this, it is essential to understand this disease completely.

ALL FOR SALE

Hard work is prerequisite to prosperity. Whoever works in a particular field becomes successful in that field.

Success brings name, fame and money. To have money and to earn money is not at all bad. But that should be legal, ethical and hard earned.

We are not able to accept the fact that hospitals charge heavily and colleges seek donations. We are still under the illusion that they are service-oriented institutions.

But now we should assimilate the fact that they are institutions started with capital investment and in return they want to earn profits which is only natural. Movies, magazines for that matter every art form today is business related.

For example if a room in an ordinary hotel costs hundred rupees a day, it may cost thousand rupees in a star hotel. The difference is due to the investment, hotel maintenance which includes service, cleanliness, bathroom facilities, class and style. Everything has a value. We have to decide whether we are ready for it or not.

When it comes to hospitals, the qualifications of doctors, their experience, modern equipment, and operation theatres with all facilities are taken into account while billing a patient. In universities their effort towards higher education has a value attached.

In this world everything is linked with money. Wherever there is money, loss and profit also count. Man cannot endure difficulties. The business man cannot accept losses.

EVERYONE LOVES TO LOVE

We usually hesitate to talk to people. While dealing with people in position we don't know where we may go wrong. So we keep distance. No doubt we should respect and be courteous to eminent people and elders. But, there is nothing to fear or to hesitate. These people are usually large hearted. They don't mind even if we commit a mistake. However great a person may be he is born like anyone else. He grows up like anyone else.

He comes up in life with discipline and perseverance. So he understands a common man. A person cannot be great if he cannot understand a common man. Suppose by mistake a person is depicted and circulated as a great one in society let us leave him alone.

We are talking about great people who are genuine. When we see them from close quarters they look very simple. They too have love, desires and some weaknesses just like us.

However serious they may be outwardly they burst into laughter once they hear a joke. However balanced they may look, they suffer like us in the face of difficulty. It is great to have that simple attitude which reacts like a child.

But when they work in the field in which they are great, they are no ordinary people. There the world can witness unusual talent and universal personality.

We can talk to any eminent person face to face without fear. As individual no one is frightening. But in their own work they are great and strong.

SHOULD LIVE LIKE A PERENNIAL RIVER

We may say something today,and may condemn the same after a while.That does not make us fickleminded.

Our views should never be like that of still water in a tank. They should resemble an ever flowing stream of a perennial river. Some people may consider this as not being "steadfast." Should we consider what we know only as great and never admit that it is wrong even when we realise that to be so? Is it called steadfastness?

To be limited to one style of thinking for ever reflects a closed mind. If we create a circle around us not to allow anything new to cross that circle adhering to the old thinking for ever is like still water in a pond.

Even the so called "intellectuals" have their heads functioning like gramophone records. Whenever you put it on, you listen to the same sounds and nothing new. For years together those "intellectuals" have same words, same thoughts and same principles. They reiterate the same old stuff. That means they are confined to those ideas in a particular mould.

The sunflower always turns to the sun. That means it always turns to light. Does it mean it is a fickleminded flower?

Fresh air can enter only when a window is kept open. Open mind alone can judge truth from untruth.

THE MIND ACCORDING TO THE AGE

Once a child entered a pipe. At the end of it was a deep ditch. The child had already reached the middle of the pipe. There was a danger of he falling into the ditch. People implored him not to go that side but to come back. He was a crawling baby who did not know the language.

Elders were very concerned. They showed him chocolates. "Come this side, this side," they persuaded. But that child did not care. He started moving towards the ditch. One wise man thought of a device. He brought another child of the same age and made him sit at the beginning of the pipe. The first child looked at this child and laughed. This one also laughed. Both of them clapped hands, looked at each other and made joyful sounds.

They conversed in their own language.

The first child who earlier headed towards the end of the pipe and the ditch came back crawling towards the second child who was at the beginning of the pipe. Every body heaved a sigh of relief. That means one child could understand another child's language. He liked it. That is why he came out of the pipe. Otherwise all the elders and their wisdom together could not draw him out.

I am narrating this to tell that we should bring up our children thinking from their point of view. We should not try to preach them big things. They will yield no results.

THEY ARE THERE SOMEWHERE

We usually dream about getting good matches to our children so that they can be happily married. Either a boy or a girl we only want them to be happy.

It is said that we should marry our daughter in a rich family and bring home a daughter-in-law from a poor family. So while talking about rich and poor families we are giving importance only to financial matters. Besides we also form certain opinions either knowingly or unknowingly.

If any young man says idealistically, "I will marry without dowry", there are many doubting Thomases who will say, "Who knows what is wrong with him."

Similarly if a beautiful young woman with money, status and good character says, "All I need is a good husband. I am not concerned with other things", there are people mean enough to say, "There is some snag here."

These sort of opinions are contradictory in themselves. The fact is there is no relationship between character and riches. All rich people are not bad.

All poor people are not great. Good and bad, good people as well as bad people are there everywhere. So we have to take into consideration only the personality of a person. If we continue to have this outlook marriage will take place at an appropriate time.

Everyone is married as destined. There is no doubt that all parents will succeed in getting suitable brides and bridegrooms for their children.

STOP SOLILOQUIES

When we are faced with difficulties and are at loss we tend to say, "Oh, I didn't think this way. I thought it would be that way." This plight is the result of we confining our thoughts to ourselves. If we start talking openly and face to face, many hardships will be removed.

We arrange the marriage of our daughter without knowing her mind.We think our liking is her liking. Later on, we regret that the girl is unhappy. That yields nothing.

Instead of keeping to ourselves, had we asked the girl before hand, this disaster could have been averted.

Similarly we imagine so many things about our friends. If we ask a friend directly, "Is it what you are thinking of me?" we will get a straight answer. Then our misunderstanding will clear and we will get mental peace. But we don't do that.

If each one of us starts thinking badly of others, the whole world will become a virtual hell.

Certain misunderstandings that arise between husband and wife belong to this category. If they talk to each other frankly, the problems will be solved. The problem arises because each one keeps to himself and lets loose one's imagination.

The tongue is not meant only for having taste buds. This is a great instrument to express our inner thoughts. Once a frank dialogue starts, even enemies will become friends.

THERE LIES BITTERNESS IN SWEET WORDS

It is very difficult to speak truth and make it agreeable. But falsehood can be uttered with smiles.

When others depict truth as untruth, those who know the truth become helpless. They converse in a calm way. We get disturbed and pained. We try to put across our point. In that confusion, we may express some anger.

Then they cajole us. As if we were committing a mistake they would say,"Please calm down. You are getting emotional."

Whenever the real point needs to be discussed, they put aside the point and talk softly and gently.

Then we really get angry. Naturally there will be mistakes.

They catch hold of that mistake and question us. They prolong the same matter.

"Just now you said that. Is it not true?" They smile. That annoys us more.

On certain occasions even to tell truth one has to shout. That is why artificial thing pleases and natural thing blows hot winds.

Some people dig our graves while speaking sweetly. Even in food, sweet things are very harmful to us.

Even when the word is harsh, mind should be soft like butter. Tempting sweet words will not serve. Only a deed that could feed a stomach is important.

MENTAL CLEANLINESS IS IMPORTANT

Many people have good habits.They get up early in the morning and go for a walk. They don't take tea or coffee. They take good food. They are away from bad habits. True. All these are necessary.

Just as exercise and good food habits are essential for physical health, good mind and heart are essential for mental health.

All those with bad habits are not bad people. One cannot be measured by one's habits.One's thinking style and one's behaviour which is worth stimulating are essential.

Some people make fun of others by saying, "I am not like him. I don't smoke. I don't drink. I don't even touch coffee."

But some have a good heart in spite of their bad habits. They have a healthy mind.Such people have love and compassion. They are useful to the world.

A person with bad habits ruins himself. He loses his own money. But the one without a healthy mind is a bad person who will ruin his street, his town, his state and his country.

So mental health is more important than physical health. Bad habits are bad anyway. We need not make a special mention of them. But it is essential to preserve our mental health along with physical health. It is our duty.

ALL-PERVADING RAMA

The running commentary on the radio only interrupts our hearing of sacred chanting at the time of Sri Rama Kalyanam at Bhadrachalam. What is the gain? What do listeners get? Atleast they should get a feeling of watching the sacred ceremony while listening to **mantras.**

We are not only disgusted with this unnecessary commentary but are also deprived of the opportunity to listen to those sacred **mantras.** Is this what we get out of radio commentary?

We depend on the running commentary of All India Radio because we are not fortunate enough to see Sri Rama's Kalyanam directly. But what we get are unwanted descriptions and comments about crowds.

We do need commentators to some extent. They should just give some introduction and leave it at that. They should not be all-pervading and obstruct the sounds of sacred chantings of the priests. Mantras related to Gouripooja and the sound of music that is played at the time of tying of sacred marriage thread along with appropriate mantras will be an enthralling experience.

They should limit their commentary and be a bridge between the audience and priests. They should bring the event live before the audience.

Sri Rama Navami is celebrated in every town and in every home. We consider Sri Rama's Kalyanam to bring about universal good.

It is said that it is good to chant Rama's name or even to hear it. How much more fortunate we would be if we could listen to the sacred chants at the time of Rama's wedding!

WE SHOULD SOCIALISE

Man is free. He can do what he wants to do. He can speak what he wants to speak. He can follow what he likes best. But instead of being free, mingling with others and be cheerful we tend to freeze all alone.

We can freely express our views. But we don't. We should listen to others point of view and can comment frankly. That should be an honest opinion.

Whatever we want to say we should do so without hesitation. Similarly we should understand what the other person is saying. But generally we do not give the other person an opportunity to talk to us freely.

We show off our importance. The attitude that we need not care for others is mainly responsible for this.

Not only that. In our heart of hearts we have a feeling that we are very organised, we have good values, lead a systematic life and are far superior to others.

We should behave in a way that everyone should be comfortable to talk to us. We should not create a fear in others that they hesitate, "We do not know how he takes it." It is always better to persuade than to create a fear in them.

Only an inefficient person thinks that one should not walk though having legs, one should not see though having eyes and one should not speak though there is a mouth. It is good to talk freely and comfortably. But listening is better than that.

GOOD ENDING

Of all fears, death is something which frightens us to death. We know that every one born has to die, yet we fear it.However great a person maybe, whatever may be the medical facilities available, whoever may be the doctors attending, if time is up one has to leave.

We wish to have an easy death without under going agonising experiences. We have to do our bit towards this. We should regulate our food and life style. We should give up those things which directly harm our health.

Is it not nice to die while having the boots on rather than to be bed-ridden waiting for death? When we know that death is inevitable, we have to be ready to face it in a natural way. The death, which treats all equal, cannot devour us alone. Why should we fear?

The life with fear is almost death-like life. There is no meaning in living in fear of death which may occur one day. The fear of death is created by mind. So it should be won over by will power.

It is better to leave the emaciated body. We feel quite relieved when we sneeze.We get relief after vomiting. We feel quite comfortable after morning ablutions. Similarly, it should be relief enough when we leave this body. Who knows?Let us invite trouble-free death.

YOU AND I ARE ALSO IMPORTANT

Hurry. Hurry. Work or talk or for everything else, there is hurry.

If it is for something good, a good deed to be done for others, one can understand the hurry. If it is beneficial to others, it does not matter if one puts in a word in a hurry. But for ordinary things also, we utter a few words in haste.

These words will hurt others. After saying that we repent, "Oh, why did we hurt that person unnecessarily?" Had we taken some care before uttering those words, how nice it would have been!

Similarly we act in haste on certain occasions. If a gate is closed at the railway crossing, we can't tolerate that. When the gate opens, we want to be the first ones to cross. So there is a lot of competition. The result is traffic jam. Everyone gets delayed.The more we are in a hurry, the more it gets delayed.

We don't like to stand in queue. We would like to jump the queue to be ahead of others. We don't think that even others are in a hurry. For us, our own work is important. We are indifferent to the needs of others. It is being very narrow-minded to think "Me first."

We don't realise that just as we feel our work is very important so also for others their work is important. It is not right to say,"Each one to himself." Every one should get their share. This is social justice and the characteristic of coexistence.

SEEING AN ELEPHANT WITH A MAGNIFYING GLASS

It has become a part of our conversation to find fault with others, to discuss bad people and to complain that this world is full of cheating and deceit.

We try to see how many people are worse than us. If we are the type who do not pay back the loan there are others who usurp someone else's property.

We curse the fellow saying, "How bad! How deceitful!" and think we are good. If someone is a liar we condemn him saying. "What a fellow, he can't speak but lies." We comfort ourselves thinking we tell lies only when there is a need.

We don't ever think about good people or noble people. We neither have an urge nor do we make an effort to be like them. Moreover we tell ourselves, "It is all right. They can afford to do all the good. Had we the opportunities and suitable conditions we could have done better."

Good nature has nothing to do with one's family or heritage. Good path is not linked with education. Generosity does not require property or status.

Whatever be our level, however limited be our scope, our inclination to do good to others is no way affected. Though we know all this, we find excuses to pursue bad. This is a great wrong. Truth, righteousness and justice are not confined to a few.

Everything should start from us. If everyone follows one's own conscience, each one can be a noble person.

PLAYING DOESN'T SPOIL

We like our children very much. But we like them within the parameters of our own liking and disliking. We don't allow the children to behave according to their taste, wishes and thoughts.

We are admitting them into convent schools even before they are weaned away from their milk bottle. Instead of being playful, they are to start their education. We are making them prisoners of books. We make them study for next year when they get their holidays. We don't allow them to enjoy. We don't notice how those little hearts are affected.

We always insist that they should like what we like. We never care to find out what they themselves like. Why that far? Do we buy play things for children? No. Why? We say they spoil them and the money is wasted. We are ready to buy something which they will eat, but toys? We don't buy.

"I don't want to eat anything. Buy me that toy", may be their refrain. We chide them. We say those toys will be broken and spoiled. Thus we nip their desire in the bud. We think it is a sheer waste of money to buy a toy which is likely to be spoiled.

Should we buy unbreakable iron toys? We are imprisoning the children and not allowing them to play. It is natural for children to play. Breaking a toy while playing is as natural as digesting food.

It is not enough if one thinks,"We are loving our children enough." We should introspect if we are nipping their unbound childhood, in the bud.

NO NEED TO FEAR

Are we devoted to God? Do we fear God? I think we fear God more than we worship him.

While walking or travelling, joining palms in reverence to each and every temple, suddenly closing eyes and praying to God are all characteristics of fear and reverence towards God.

Should one join palms whenever one sees a temple or an idol? Will God be angry if we do not greet him? Is God meant only to frighten us? No. It is not correct.The one who frightens can never be God. God gives assurance. He protects a believer as well as a non-believer.

If we do not have complete faith which says, "God is within us, with us. He is omnipresent", this sort of frightened reverence can only increase fear. Let us put an end to these fears and weaknesses. Let us visit God without any fear.

When we return home after travelling, we feel a lot of happiness. With similar happiness we should enter a temple. We should enter a temple with the type of love we have for children and the kind of reverence we have for our parents.

Threatening, punishing... these are not deeds of God. If we do good, we have good returns. If we do bad, we have bad results. There is no interference of God in these matters.

Just as it is meaningless to fear our own shadow, it is purposeless to fear a temple and the God in the temple.

LET THERE BE NO DOUBT IN LOVE

We love so many people. Many more people love us.But in between we are beleaguered by meaningless doubts. If anyone loves us, we get so many doubts as, "Is it real love? Or is it pretension? Is it permanent or temporary?"

With this kind of argument, we doubt the very people who love us. As a result, we keep others at a distance. If we start distancing ourselves from everyone, we can't love anybody or get anybody's love. It is futile to look for permanence in love. It is enough if we drink water when we are thirsty. It is enough if we get love when we need it.

Why to ask for permanent love when we ourselves are not permanent. It is not proper to think, "He is cheating us. His love is false. He is loving with some other motive."

When we accept the love of the other person, there should be no place for doubt.One should receive it then and there. It is unnecessary whether it is real or false. He is loving us and we too should love him. Our thoughts should be limited to this.

We should not calculate, "How much love are we getting from others? What is its depth? How long will it last?" The one who does not love will never love.If we start doub-ting the one who loves and scrutinise, we are left to ourselves devoid of love.

WE ARE IMPORTANT TO OURSELVES

We undergo a lot of difficulties in life. We work for so many purposes. In the bargain, we are giving up our own comfort. We consider indulging in small pleasures as selfish and unnecessary.

We hesitate to spend money which we have earned. Though the entire money is not meant for spending, at least some percentage should be spent on personal comfort.

We know the usefulness of money. A part of it is for savings, a part of it is for necessities and a little is for our pleasures. After spending on pleasures, we start repenting, "Oh, we have spent it unnecessarily." Infact, we hesitate to spend. We save our money as if it were someone else's. What is the point of having money which cannot be spent on our comfort.

We struggle to save everything we earn.We don't understand the purpose of money.From thrift, we are moving towards stinginess. If we spend reasonably, there is pleasure in earning.

If we earn hundred rupees, we must spend atleast ten rupees towards our pleasure. Then we should think we have earned only ninety rupees. If one cannot spend, one cannot earn also. If one cannot work hard, there will be no earning. Our life is meant for hard work.

We should enjoy money, prosperity and the pleasures we get out of them. We should share them with our own people.

THE MIND ALWAYS THINKS

We get so many thoughts that there is always a flow. Sometimes there are good thoughts,sometimes there are bad thoughts.

When we get bad thoughts, we feel bad. "Why did I think like this? What a bad thought!" All this conflict is a waste.

Our mind always gallops like a horse and it is natural to think, with the same speed.

Mind is meant for thinking. If we try to control, there is only pain and nothing more. Mind runs is different ways and with limitless speed. No machine or a charm can have that speed. So there is no need to control such a great power. If anyone asks you to control your thoughts, that means you have to live like a dead person.

Thinking is not a crime. No thought is bad. But trying to suppress thoughts is wrong.

We should have an attitude to look at thoughts as they are without subjecting ourselves to anxiety. If not, we will be afraid even to think.

It is enough if we are careful while implementing our thoughts. One should not feel that thinking itself is wrong. While implementing a thought one should make use of one's intellect. Let us give freedom to our mind.When it comes to taking a decision, let us be cautious. There is no need to be anxious at the time of thinking.At the time of implementation, care is needed.

ALL LIMBS ARE EQUAL

All parts of our body are important. We can't neglect the left eye because we have the right eye. Can we breathe with one nostril? Should we confine listening to only one ear? When we give importance to all parts of our body, why do we look down on our left hand? So also we down grade left leg. Why do we look down on ourselves with meaningless sentiments?

Why should we have contempt for left hand? We have to face great discomfort without that. If we lose one of the hands, we will not be able to perform many tasks.

We say, "Nothing should be given with left hand. Everything should be accepted with right hand." How unjust! So also we say, "One should not put left leg forward." Why? What happens if left leg is put forward? Are we walking with only one leg? Can we?

Unfortunately there are many handicapped people. We are witnessing their problems. When we have all our limbs in order, neglecting a few of them is nothing but ignorance.

We cannot discriminate between our children. All are equal to us. Similarly all parts of body are important. Each one has its own role.

The day we realise this, we will stop discriminating between parts of body and down grading ourselves.

NO BEGINNING AND NO END FOR A WHEEL

Apart from riches and status, at every home, every person has some task or the other that needs completion.

There is no way to say, "I have done all my work. I have no dissatisfaction." Though what we achieved gives us satisfaction a feeling always remains that there is something more to do.

At home also there may be a fan which is not working. At another place there is a switch with loose connection. One chair has only three legs crying for repair. Even the dresses we wear have something lacking–a hole in a pocket or a missing button.

This way there is no perfection or completion. Yet it is important to do our duty well according to our capacity and as far as our mind cooperates. It is better to be cool with satisfaction than to live with burning dissatisfaction.

We should be happy when a day's work is done. Otherwise we have to suffer dissatisfaction and mental unrest. Then we also lose the capacity to be happy about our earlier achievement.

If we can really think and feel that we have done as much as we could, that works as a tonic for us to do more. When the sun sets today he has the task of rising again. That eternal light alone gives life to all beings in this creation.

ADVICE IS FOR THOSE WHO HEED

Many people seek our advice on many occasions. But they don't heed our advice. So, it is waste to advise them.

Normally those who seek advice come to us after forming their own opinion. If our advice does not support their view, they don't listen to us.

That means they seek our advice only to get their opinion strengthened but not to follow our advice.

All this is happening because there is no open-mindedness. If they get a negative reply from us, they just dismiss our words. They justify themselves by giving many reasons. They try to make us agree with them.

If we are inclined towards their opinion, they are at peace.

Even if we don't agree with their decision and express our own opinion, they do what they have already decided. So this ritual of seeking advice is self-deceit.

The one who seeks advice should receive the other man's thinking in proper perspective. He should think of pros and cons. Keeping his ego aside, he should judge his own opinion. When one cannot do that, why should one approach us for advice?

We are humiliated by giving advice to such people. It is waste of time for both the parties. Why to give advice and then get into problems? Why should we be hurt if they do not pay heed to our advice?

A GOOD TURN HAS NO BAD MEANING

Now-a-days, there is none who will not borrow. This is a social necessity. It is a humanitarian deed for a person with money to lend to someone who is in need. That is kind-heartedness.

We need money very badly. Then we don't get a loan from anywhere. Some cannot lend because they don't have. Others don't want any further trouble, so they don't give.At this juncture someone lends money and helps us. We are able to overcome our hardship. We express our gratitude by saying, "I can never forget this good you have done." This is very well. As time passes, our gratitude diminishes. Besides, we start doubting the other person's motive.

"Well, when no one else was prepared to lend the money, why did this one give?" we ask ourselves. Then we conclude, "He has some purpose. He needs our help somewhere. That is why he lent the money so readily not because he was generous."

Then we pay him back the money. When we are in need again,we approach him again not with humility. We consider it as our right. Then he will say, "No!" That shocks us. Since he has upset us, we do false propaganda. Thus we lose this opportunity and regret later. All this is because we attributed selfish motive to the one who helped us. We should understand a good heart and fold our palms in gratitude to those who help us in need.

HERO DESERVES PLACE OF HONOUR

We experience hardships and comforts in our own way. It may sound strange, but at times we may mistake hardship as comfort and live happily.

Or one can mistake comfort to be hardship thus making one's own life a hell. For these feelings,experiences and forbearance, apart from mental attitude, differences in financial status also contribute.

Recently I witnessed an old man hammering at a concrete slab. His finger was hurt and he was bleeding. Yet he was continuing with his work. I said, "Stop the work. Let us attend to your wound first." "I didn't notice the blood till you mentioned," he replied with a smile. I did some first aid for him.

He said, "Leave it, sir, why this fuss? It will be all right soon. Even otherwise I will not give any comfort to this wound." So many meanings were there to his words. So many thoughts came to my mind.

Apart from taking it lightly he made one more point. People like us would normally rush to the doctor. He cleanses, applies medicine, bandages the wound almost like performing a surgery.

That means we gave a lot of importance to that wound. So according to the old man we have given comfort to the wound. Sensitive mind is good but a sensitive body does not give us comfort.

WE ALSO GET OLD

We crave very much for children. When we get children, we look after them very well. We pin so many hopes on them. But we forget that even our parents loved us so much. Once we have our own family, that becomes our world and our life.

In our anxiety to shape our children's future, we neglect our parents. There is nothing wrong in working hard for children's future. That is essential. But there is no reason why parents should be left out.

Parents bring up their children even if they are many in number. They never for once think, "How to feed so many children?" Irrespective of their economic condition,parents bring up children with loving care.

But even one among the ten children does not look after the old parents. They consider it as a great burden to look after the parents. Parents are considered as an obstacle to lead a happy life. This is cruel.

Suppose our children neglect us so in future, then what of us? Even if we realise the pain and the hopelessness our parents have undergone, what does it matter?

Old parents have to depend on somebody physically and economically. Children should look after them. But what are the children doing?

When we comprehend the future consequences, we will be able to understand the agony of our parents.

SPIRITUAL RELATIONSHIP NEEDED

We are very fond of our relatives. "Friendship is my life. Friends are very important,"we may say. But there is not much truth in that. Sometimes we feel, "Relatives are like vultures.They devour us but never come forward to help." But when time comes, we know it is relatives who come for help.

For anything good or bad that happens at our home and in society, we give priority to relatives. But what about the friendship? We go to friends at the time of need and see our necessities are met.

Whenever someone wants to have love marriage, normally, the family does not agree. All the relatives support the family. They don't attend the marriage. There are occasions when the newly weds have been excommunicated. On such occasions, friends see to it that the marriage takes place. But relatives and parents show contempt for the couple.

Gradually the relatives start dropping in at the lover's den. Then they praise. "You have taken a bold step. Very good. You are an ideal couple."

With this, they are flattered, "Anyway, relatives are relatives. How can outsiders be our own?" In this emotional upsurge, they forget the friends who arranged the marriage. They become secondary.

"Blood is thicker" theory is recalled. One should not discriminate between relatives and friends. What is essential is development of mental relationship but not more and more relationships.

YES, MAN IS NOT SEASONAL

We all have our own character, our own method and our own conviction. At times we feel perhaps we should change to make others comfortable. We try to change but do not succeed. Then we are in agony worrying why we are not able to change.

The world understands us in a particular way. Some accept us and others reject us. But we crave for acceptance from everyone. This is unnecessary because no one in this world is acceptable to all.

If one thinks one thing is bad there is another who thinks that it is good. If our aim is to be called good by those who called us bad then we have to settle for being called bad by those who called us good.

This circle is unending. Our personality is our own. Our character is our own. There are no decisive factors to decide what is good or what is bad. The cowardice of a cat and ferocity of a lion are their natural traits.

They cannot be exchanged nor will they try for that. We also view these animals as they are. We become wild seeing one and get frightened seeing the other.

This world comes to know what we are by means of our actions. Let us be so. If we kill our natural trait and try to imitate others we will certainly become a laughing stock.

They ridicule us saying after all what is so great about you. So let us not change. Let us be ourselves. If a crocodile is displaced it becomes a plaything for children. If we give up our natural traits we will not be counted as anything. So let us be ourselves.

THERE IS GOOD IN BAD AND BAD IN GOOD

We keep a target and strive to achieve it. Generally we reach the target we aimed at.On certain occasions we fail due to some reasons. Then we are disappointed. We feel as if we had lost everything in life.

There are many fields. There are many ways. If one has determination to achieve, one can shine in any field.

Why should we consider only a particular field as great? Why should we think that the fields other than what we wanted are inferior?

Everything is great and everyone is efficient.

Some students want to become doctors. Some others want to be engineers. Does it mean the rest of the students have dark future? Not at all. For the one who has been defeated, there is yet another way destined.

When there is another field waiting for you where you can shine, you face defeat in this field. It is but natural to be pained when faced with defeat. One thinks that one has been hurt along with the members of the family. So one feels sad. One has to get over this.Today's pain will not last till tomorrow. Sometimes what we consider as beneficial may be harmful. The job we do, since there is no other way, may prove to be wonderful. Victory is not the last step in life. Defeat does not put an end to future.Our life is an endless journey with an admixture of victory and defeat.

GOOD EXPERIENCE IS GREAT

Generally, we don't care for the advice of the elders and the words that come out of their experience. We question if it would happen even in our case and do what we are forbidden to do.Why cannot it be good? Thinking thus, we go upstream and get hurt in the process. Then only wisdom dawns. We try to dissuade others but they may also like to have a taste of their own experience and may get hurt.

We continue to live with hurts but never leave the bad behind. We don't hold on to the good. If everyone takes their own chance, the words of elders and the lessons of their experience become futile.

We may have self-confidence. To certain extent, it is essential.

It is good to go ahead with adventure.But it should not result in misadventure and overconfidence.

We may win where others have been defeated.But we should know why they have been defeated. We should leave that defeating point and start our journey towards victory. We should not start from the beginning. If we do so, we will bite the dust. Similarly we should know the secret of those who are victorious. We should understand how far we can adopt that.

This is where we need discretion. When something good is said, why should we hesitate to accept it? We should emulate whatever is good. It is not correct to think that we are always right. No one is omniscient and that includes us as well.

WE SHOULD LOOK AT THOSE MOMENTS WHICH WILL NOT RETURN

We dream of arranging grand marriages for our children. We make many efforts. We plan it years ahead and save money. We try every source to gather information regarding a good alliance.

At long last, our efforts yield results. We start making arrangements for the marriage. We undergo hardship, spend a lot of money, more than we can afford and celebrate the marriage. All these are very fine. But we are not able to witness our children's marriage from close quarters.

The children's marriage ceremony which is the most important thing in our life is not witnessed by us. We are leaving this to video cameras. We are busy in welcoming friends and relatives, and in seeing them off.

Inspite of all the precautions we take,there may be something lacking somewhere in the arrangements. Then we feel sorry about it and think, "I wish I had taken more care."

Well,whatever you may do, someone or the other will point out a flaw. That does not matter. The thing to be concerned about is how unfortunate it is not to witness our children's marriages to our heart's content.

More than the grand arrangements we make for a marriage, the marriage itself is important. Looking after the guests should be left to some of our people. These are the moments when our life's ambition is being fulfilled.

Our children's marriage ceremony should be witnessed with peace and happiness. There is no greater happiness than this.

DISCHARGING DUTY IS ENOUGH

It is a mistake to think that everything is perfect. We should take enough care as far as possible. One should not be lazy or indifferent to work. But one should not go to the extreme.

Some people don't take anything seriously. They are not careful about anything. Even when things are crossing the danger mark, these people are stable without moving an inch. They don't even do their bit of work. This is a strange behaviour. No good will come out of it to himself or to his family. He will remain a useless person.

It is also wrong to take everything seriously and to strive to avoid the slightest mistake or flaw. If we want anything to be perfect, our single effort will not do.We need many people's co-operation.But we cannot direct that they should work like us. How can our work be as important to others as it is to us? It is also wrong to think that way. Each one will have his own method. It is desirable to adapt ourselves to their method rather than expecting others to adopt our method.

Striving towards perfection is good.But it should not become an obsession. One has to compromise a little. Otherwise so much time will be wasted that in a big work one has to face several defects. Perfection should be only a method and it should not be madness.

HAVE NO ENVY

Everyone has emotions.Some are prone to anger. Some have lust. Some others have arrogance. Yet others have envy. This way there is some bad element or the other in everyone. Some of these are intertwined with human life and become part of day to day living. Even if one of these characteristics is high, it harms the person as well as the society.

The one who is burning with envy will not differentiate between one person and another. He doesn't care if the other person is his relative or friend. If an actor is shooting to fame, this one may be envious. If any other person is gaining fame, this one may be burning with envy. There is no reason for his envy.

If someone near by is prospering, one may feel envy. To some extent one may understand this. But to be envious about a person with whom we have no concern is very unfortunate. This indeed is an incurable disease. The fellow will for ever suffer with this disease.

He will be talking ill of the person at as many places as possible. He writes anonymous letters and says harsh things to hurt the person. The coward may get some relief out of it. If no one pays attention, he himself may become miserable. If we continue to smile in front of the person who longs for our unhappiness, that will serve him right and make him more miserable.

ONE SHOULD DISTRIBUTE THE RESULT OF LABOUR

Unless one works hard, one cannot survive in this world. One has to work very hard. There is no other way. We are afraid that this hard work may affect our health. But hard work does not affect the body. The more we do physical work, the better we will be. The more we do mental work, the sharper the mind will be.

But we get anxious of work. If we do any work with anxiety, it will not be completed. We are treating anxiety as part of work. So we are facing obstacles in work.

We some times pity our ownselves saying, "Oh we are working very hard." We tell the same to others and try to get their sympathy. A hard-working person does not need anybody's sympathy. He does not need anybody's support. He does not get into any difficulties.

The secret of good health is in hard work. In fact, it is fortunate to have an opportunity to work hard. But the labour we choose should have a direction and a method. If we spend time with purposeless work, then indeed it is pitiable.

If we exclude a few great people who work only for the welfare of the society, most of us work hard only for ourselves. We may think, "I want to improve my lot. So I work hard. What is wrong in that?" Nothing wrong in that. The only thing is our improvement should not cause harm to others.

ADDRESSING PROPERLY

We change our cloak according to the occasion. We change our language depending on the situation. These changes are not permanent. They are not real. Just to get our work done and to have our purpose served, these changes are made.

Why, we address the other person in many ways. Depending on our necessity, we address him "Sir", for every sentence. If we think that it is not very important, we will say, "All right, what is it?" If the other person is in no way useful to us, our stature grows higher.

"What nonsense, what is it? Say it fast. I have other things to do." We forget we addressed the same person, "Sir" and got our work done.

We are under the wrong notion that we are very intelligent and can trap others easily. We don't know that given an opportunity, everyone is a capable person. May be, today the other person must be asking a favour from us. Where is the guarantee that we will not be in that situation one day?

It is sheer arrogance to address a person contemptuously and derogatorily. It is him we addressed as "Sir" not long ago. If the other person is noble, our method of addressing does not affect him. He would neither gain nor lose.

We should address each one according to his values, but not according to our needs.

GOOD MULTIPLIES

We all need each other's help. We should get what we want from others and do what they want from us. No one can come up in life without anybody's help. From dawn to dusk everyday, we need the help of several people. We seek their co-operation and get benefitted. Similarly, we should be useful to others when they need us and we should not hesitate.

Suppose a person who refused to do us a favour comes to us requesting for a favour, we should forget about the past and do whatever good we can. So we get a lot of satisfaction that we did good to a person who harmed us. The other person will remember the past and will be ashamed.

He acknowledges our good deed with gratitude.

Just as there is more water as we draw, so also we get benefitted even more if we help others.

Anger and annoyance should be temporary. It is not good to have lifelong enmity.

Since we are ordinary people,we may have enmities. But they should be nipped in the bud. One should not let them grow. There may be some who accept milk and return poison.But the ultimate victory is that of a good person.

If we wish others well on ten occasions, at least once we may get benefitted.At least for our own sake, we should wish others well.

HERE AND NOW

We want others to recognise us, respect us and be around us. We are eager to be known as great people. We are disappointed when we can't get what we want.

The past, the present and the future determine greatness. A person who is great in all times is indeed great. A person who is great only at one point of time cannot be counted as great. Our people are also like that.

Whatever is done is done and whatever is given is given. They start asking you might have given then, what about now. We are all ever hungry type.

When it comes to future they don't care. "Who knows when you can become great. Let us see if you are great now," they may say.

So it is a waste to worry about this kind of name and fame. If we spend our time struggling for useless things we are left with the question, "What did I achieve?"

Suppose we become great in a particular field and get recognition we cannot move about freely.

Then life becomes narrow. We have to think twice before doing anything. All eyes are on us. All ears strain to listen what we say.

This way we are chaining our own freedom. It is better to be behind the screen which gives us a lot of freedom. We can do many things. We can achieve many things.

So let us not expect any greatness and let there be no regret that we could not become great. We should continue with our daily duty. Let us not be one apart, let us be one among many.

ONE HARSH WORD AND EVERY THING ELSE IS FORGOTTEN

"If you like us, we will be happy. You give your money, we will accept it happily. You look after us, we will be comforted. Get jobs for our unemployed children, we will think that you have done a great deal for us.

Get free education for our children, we consider you as a very generous person. Financially help us in our children's marriage, we will declare you as a presiding elder at the marriage. Get us houses, we will live securely in them.

But- if you express your irritation-we can't stand that. If you say a harsh word, we will not put up with it. Just because you have certain responsibility, should you interfere with every matter? You may say that your advice is meant for our good. We know that much and this you should know. You chide our children thinking that they are spoiled. Do you think you love our children better than we ourselves love them?

You may say you have done so much for our children and for us. But we never requested you to do all that. You did it on your own. By the way, if you have not done all this, do you think we would have died or we would have starved to death? Even we have self respect. Should we be forever grateful to you?"

These are the present day conditions.

It looks better to be pretentious and do harm instead of chiding, out of love.

This is the justice of the man of today.

WE KNOW GOOD OR BAD

The statement given by so called intellectuals and creative people are confusing us on many occasions. They say something and do something else. We don't know what is truth and what is to be followed.

Those who sing for cinemas say in their public utterings thus,"The literature in cinema songs had deteriorated.Sex literature is on the increase.So audience should boycott sex films."These are the very people who sing those sex songs and these are the people who urge us in public meetings to boycott the films.

Same is the case with so called great writers. They write spicy things for money and fame. But in public forums they voice their concern, "Today's writers are corrupt. They are misleading the readers."

The editors of the magazine are no less. They state that their magazines only are family magazines and the rest of the magazines increase their circulation by sex literature. Yet they surreptitiously try to win readers by including sex in their contents.

Those who abuse the thing that gives them livelihood and fame are infact cutting the branch of the tree on which they are sitting. No notice should be taken of such words. We should follow our own way. We should listen to what pleases us, should see what we like and should read what appeals to us.

DON'T COMPETE WITH NEIGHBOURS

Demand for apartments is a recent phenomenon. Apartments provided accommodation to many. They have become house holders. An opportunity is provided for people to live together.

Contacts increased. Friendship prospered. The world of knowledge widened. There is a great opportunity to share knowledge. Good conventions like sharing joys and sorrows, exchanging gifts are on the increase.

But this is only one aspect.On the other hand something harmful is happening. Comparing oneself with the others is increasing. competition with neighbours has started.

We are curious to know what are the things they have in their housc, what kind of furniture, what brands of television, fridge and stereo and start feeling unhappy if we do not have the same.

We started craving for more modern comforts than our neighbours. To fulfil these increasing demands we need money. One is not hesitant to adopt wrong ways to earn money.

Just as one person cannot be like another in physical form, one family cannot be like another family in status, responsibilities, income and expenditure. One should not court hardships by trying to live beyond one's means.

We should try to emulate whatever is good in our neighbours. We should compete with their personalities and not with their material possessions.

LOOK THROUGH MY EYE!

Every creature in the creation is beautiful.But we consider some as 'ugly'. Everyone is beautiful in a mirror. The concept of beauty varies according to the person who sees. Beauty is in the mind of a person who sees and in the bright rays that the mind emits.

The thing that is ugly for us, may be extraordinarily beautiful for others. Every creature is beautiful in one angle or the other.

The inner eye is better than the outer eye. This view alone can see the real beauty. If one cannot see such beauty, that becomes a partial view. We can not decide beauty with a partial view and partiality. If definition or measures or statistics are demarcated for beauty, then crores of people will feel miserable thinking they are very ugly. Or they may be extraordinarily proud of their beauty. But is it happening that way? No.

For each one, his companion looks beautiful. It gives happiness. There is no compromise on this. Truly, the couples are living a happy and contented life. That is why there are no scales to measure beauty.

There are many couples who are living happily though they are born blind. There are friends though both of them are blind. What is the outer beauty that is binding them? They have an inner eye which helps them to see each other. That is what is binding them permanently.

It is better to have mental eye that can see the mind than to have eyes which are blind to this.

IF WE REMEMBER OUR COMING TOGETHER, THERE IS NO PARTING

Some people meet. They go about together. Within a few months, they know each other well. When their ideas differ, they separate. No one should be faulted. But if we take long standing associations into consideration, how do such close relationships turn sour and we consider each other as enemies?

We know of couples who live together for years and later seek divorce. The partners who started their business with one idea are divided with so many conflicts and become enemies to each other.

Why is it happening? Why are the opinions changing completely? Where is the defect? All are doubts, but there is only one answer. When a person thinks he has no need of the other person, they separate. So only our necessities are bringing us together. There are no affections or attachments. If so, things would not have been like this.

If we ask anybody why it happened so, they will say, "I too have self-respect. Should I listen to all sorts of nonsense? Should I be doing bad things just because he asks me?"

It is all right. Then why did he bear all those bad things for so long and so many years? For that, there is no reply.

If necessity alone is bringing people together, all we have are quarrels and separations.

MAKE MINUS A PLUS

There is no end to thoughts that crop up in our mind. Some thought or the other bothers us incessantly.

In fact we can't say we are restless because of problems. Even if there is no problem or difficulty we continue with our meaningless thoughts. We think our life is full of unhappiness.

The root cause of all this is our inability to be happy. Irrespective of the fact whether a person is rich or poor everyone has something to worry. We are not clear why we should have so many worries and why do we need them.

It is our mind's tendency to wander. In a minute it can enter space and the next moment it can be on the ground.One moment it is happy recollecting good things in life and the next moment it turns into an ocean of grief reliving difficult times.

This mind which is so powerful has certain weakness also. It cannot experience happiness and unhappiness simultaneously.We should turn it into a boon. If we always fill our heart with happiness then grief has no vacancy in that.

If we come to a conclusion that there is no happiness in life then indeed we are deprived of happiness.

On the contrary if we develop an optimistic view that this life is full of happiness and we are here in this world only to experience happiness our life will certainly be an abode of happiness.

BENEFIT AND THE BENEFACTOR

Every person has to seek somebody's help at some time or the other.

Usually by give and take works out well for both. It is possible one single person may change our life totally and elevate our standard. He might have converted us a mere zero into hundred.

In that case we have to be indebted to him lifelong. Since we got so much benefit from him we intend to be grateful to him. But after sometime that gratitude feels like a burden.

We are very uncomfortable to meet him. We evade him thinking every time we meet him we should be humble before him. Why so far?

Even when we visit a temple, after seeing the deity we don't like to stay there for long. We feel comfortable only when we are out of the temple. The craving for a view of the deity and the rich experience we had before the deity which should have been treasured within us starts disappearing.

Why is it so? Why are we doing this? One thing comes out clearly. The key element is reluctance to be dependent and craving to be independent.This is the reason why children are distancing themselves from parents and people are forgetting those who helped them.

Though an ungrateful person should be considered as a burden to the earth itself, the fact of the matter is, a person who does not harm the person from whom he got the benefit is rated as the best person. We should alienate a person who says "Everything is for me" and embrace a person who says, "This is for you and me."

QUENCHING THIRST WITH SWEAT

It is natural for a man to desire to live a comfortable life. But how does one get that comfort? For that one has to work hard. His happiness is when he reaps the fruit of his hard work.

If one combines brains with brawn one can achieve many things. Though everyone knows this generally we don't like to work hard. It is wrong to expect results the moment we start working. That is greediness.

Under no circumstances one should yield to laziness, disappointment or despair. These will create a lot of disinterest in us and become obstacles to our existence itself.

All minds are alike. But like a horse the mind behaves according to the rider. If we ride it with determination we will reach our goal. It may be business or it may be a job or it can be anything.

Whatever one is doing one should reach the heights in it. Once we are there money, influence and honour will come on their own.

Progress and development are characteristics of human life. Hard work and luck work as resources. The saying that hard work yields good results and eliminates want is not baseless.

Is there anything in this world a determined mind cannot achieve? Can a person who has trust in God go astray? Same is the case with the person who has faith in hard work. There may be ups and downs but ultimate victory belongs to them.

Let us have intention and inclination to achieve success. Then it will be known that a person who reaches great heights will have more heights to reach.

THE EARTH IS FLAT FOR HIM

We take many precautions to preserve our health. We take extreme care of our body. We pay attention to each and every part of our body and are also deeply attached.

But these are not defects. This attitude does not harm anyone. Recently a person asked me with visible irritation, "What is this propaganda? Why are they appealing for donation of eyes?"

I replied, "What is wrong with that? After our death our eyes will be useful to someone else. It is a noble deed and our eyes continue to live after us."

He objected to that. "You are mistaken.If I give away my eyes and go to the other world won't the creator be annoyed with me? Won't He ask, 'I sent you as a complete man with all parts in tact. Why did you donate your eyes, as if they were your property?' Later on I will be sent to hell. I cannot undergo the torture there. Besides I shall be committing a sin if I donate anything that is given to me by God."

Oh! What logic I wondered. He was a well educated person. Before I could convince he left me in a huff.

We have many superstitions and are afraid to get rid of them. The above incident really surprised me.While we are alive we are not inclined to give anything in charity.The fact that we want to be secure even after death only shows the height of our ignorance which is indeed shameful.

MONEY AND MORALS ARE FRIENDS

Excepting a few detached persons, all of us are crazy about money. We always yearn for it. We think money is the ultimate. We do everything keeping money at the centre.

When we cannot gain money we say, "Money is very bad. It will make you do so many bad things." If we are in a position to earn money we say, "Money is goddess of wealth. One without money is useless in this world."

Each one loves his own money. There is nothing wrong in that.We do wrong things because we consider that the value of our rupee is hundred paise and the other person's rupee is worth only ten paise.

As I get remuneration for my labour, even the other person gets remuneration for his labour. So the rupee has the same value wherever it is. You may long for long, yet the other person's money would not be yours. If we work hard, we will surely get the returns.

Even our beliefs, principles and values are changing according to money. We preach a different set of principles when we do not have money. We propagate yet another set of principles when we have money. Principles should not change according to money. If a man's behaviour is the same whether he has money or no money, he will get a lot of happiness in life. If he is different at different times, then he will be ever impoverished in spite of all the wealth. Life-giving drop of potable water is always better than an ocean which cannot quench the thirst.

DON'T NEGLECT YOUR LIFE PARTNER

Sometimes we humiliate women. We look down on them. We think they are second class citizens. We don't recognise the importance of wife who is a life partner. Instead of considering her as the queen of the house, we treat her as a maid.

We don't realise that she is like a mother looking after us and our children. We don't understand that God has created housewife as his own substitute. We neglect her. If something happens and she dies, we cry in despair.A woman punishes her husband severely when she dies as a wife. There will be a vacuum which can never be filled.

While motherless children become orphans, a wifeless husband loses his support.He will be a "widower." That is why the separation from wife is considered as a great grief. It looks as if a wife is dependent on her husband. But the fact is, a husband is helpless without his wife. That is why a woman can lead her life all right even after losing husband but the man who loses his wife really becomes a destitute. One should behave keeping this truth in mind. There is no point in crying on the day she dies.One should see that she does not cry while she is alive.

Whatever may be the differences, quarrels and disputes, it is only the relationship of husband and wife that will last lifelong. We do not stay with our parents. Our own children will leave us. Everyone goes their own way. But only the wife remains as companion.

There may be several partners in business and trade but the wife stays with you all through your life.

GET RID OF ENTANGLEMENTS

Before we decide what we want and what we do not want, what is good and what is not good in our life, our birth, growth and death are taking place. Suppose today we think something is good we long for it. We work hard to achieve it. At long last we achieve it.

Then something strange happens. Should we not feel happy when we get what we want? No. We don't do that. "There is not much to it. The other one should be better.

" So we invite another desire.As soon as the new desire is born we forget to experience the happiness of our previous achievement. Our craving starts for the new thing.

We also think what we achieved in the first place is not the right thing. If only this new ambition is fulfilled we are sure to be happy the rest of our life.

Well, this ambition is also fulfilled. Still there is some dissatisfaction left. "In fact there is one more. Suppose I get victory in that there is nothing but rest in my life." So third programme too gets going.

When the third one is completed, the fourth one crops up and then the fifth one. This way there are endless desires, thoughts and tasks in our life.

There should be a difference between stomach and mind. We have a sumptuous breakfast. Yet by afternoon we feel hungry.

Hunger can never be satisfied. But mind should not be so. There should not be a continuous chain of desires. Life becomes meaningful only when we recognise what we have achieved and experience the happiness to go forward.

SAY AUSPICIOUS THING

Why do we have fear? Why do we get suspicious that others may harm us or something bad may happen. Because basically we do not have trust. We don't trust human being. We don't trust the work we are doing.

We don't trust the forthcoming result. We don't trust something good can happen. So everything is full of mis-trust.

Even with two legs in tact one doubts whether he can walk. Though there are two eyes he doubts whether he can see properly. If some one asks why he is getting such doubts he has no answer.

Fear. Fear. Fear that something bad may happen. The mind says there is no danger but the heart always moves towards doubt and danger. No courage. No faith.

Why is this unfortunate situation? Is it our destiny or culmination of our sin? No, not at all. No destiny is chasing us. Nor did we commit any sin. This is all self-inflicted. Everything is in our hand. Everything is in our mind.

If we live with negative attitude we start hating our own life. We start hating our own selves. Nobody is responsible for this.

When we live with positive thoughts everything works out well in life. The world appears to be good and we start loving ourselves. A person who can see the world as it is faces no hesitation in life.

AS THE FATHER SO THE SON

We do not follow certain traditions. We do not give up certain habits and addictions. We never change our attitudes. Our conduct is our own. But we want our children to live a better life than our own. There comes a problem.

It is good to desire that we should be able to mould our children to be better than us. Then how are we practising it? It is good to divert their attention from our bad habits.

But they learn from us.They inherit our good as well as bad traits. If we lead an idealistic life they also grow up to be good citizens.

If we just say, "I didn't study. But you should study well" children do not understand.We should explain to them the hardships we encountered because we did not have education. We should tell them what we have lost in life for being a spendthrift.

We should tell them how addictions ruined our health and the price we had to pay for it. We should give them suitable examples so that they can decide for themselves.

If we tend to force them from their childhood to acquire something which we ourselves could not, there is a danger of they hating us.

Whether young or old, irrespective of their age, if we frankly share our thoughts with those who are dear to us, they too can understand our feelings.

Accordingly they adjust their behaviour and develop the way we expect them to develop. A mere advice without practice will not register. A chisel shapes a stone into a statue. Our deeds shape our children to be better persons.

MINE IS MINE, YOURS IS YOURS

There are all types of people in the society. Each one has different mentality. Each one has different way. Each one is interested in his own existence. There is nothing wrong in this. But it is wrong to have one law while receiving and yet another law while returning. There should be the same principle either for accepting or returning. But it is not happening that way.

I have a friend. Everyone says he is a good person. He owns a bicycle. He lends it to anyone who asks for it. A friend of his who used to make use of his bicycle freely, purchased his own bicycle. One day, this person's bicycle was not in working condition. So he asked the friend who is owning the new bicycle whether he could lend the bicycle.

He immediately said, "No, I will not lend."This one was shocked."What is this!I have given you my bicycle several times. I asked you only for once and you say you will not lend,"he asked.For that, the one who purchased the bicycle recently replied, "You lent your bicycle to everyone, so also to me. There is nothing special about it. I decided not to lend my bicycle to anybody. That is why I won't lend it to you also."

All those who heard him were shocked. They decried him. But he replied,"No I didn't do any wrong. It was his nature to lend his bicycle to everyone. It is my nature not to lend my bicycle to anyone."

This is how some people behave. They are ready to accept things with ten hands but when it comes to giving, they are handicapped even without single hand.

COEXISTING WITH OTHER CREATURES

To declare that someone is great, one need not undermine the other. But we always compare to say something is great. To say that a lotus is great, we lookdown on its origin. To say a cuckoo is great, we compare it with a crow. We look down on the crow forgetting that the cuckoo grew up in crow's nest.

There are so many creatures which are coexisting with us. That is natural. Having a cat, a dog, rats,cockroaches, ants etc., in our house is a clear indication to the fact that our house is prosperous.

If we have nothing to eat, none of these things will be around. We don't understand this. We drive away the cat. We kill the rat. We chase the dog. Why are we so intolerant? They also have a right to coexist with us.

When a crow caws, we chase it away.We are afraid that guests may pester us. But while performing last rites of our elders, we invite the crow.If crows do not respond and do not accept our offering, we feel guilty. Then we see our ancestors in the crows. If a crow touches our offering we feel as if our ancestors have accepted. What is this paradox?

The crow which is normally condemned by us is treated as our ancestor.We quote our **shastras.** But **shastras** never change. It is our attitude which changes. It is not enough if a householder coexists with humanbeings. He should coexist with the other fellow creatures. That is the real householder's life.

PEOPLE LYING IN HEAPS

Creation is endless. There are billions of living beings. Among all these the one who can change and should change is human being alone. No other creature has any change in its life.They die the way they are born.This is the law of creation.

Only human being has intellect. We see many things, read many things and hear many things.All these help us as tools.They are the ways to progress from bad to good and from good to nobility. But we are closing all doors. Whatever we have seen, read or heard is not entering our mind.

A hill near a sea withstands the impact of the sea and its waves and remains unchanged. Even man is no different. Though he can move and make others move has changed his heart into a stone. He continues to repeat his mistakes which he did in his twenties, forties and sixties.

When we say man will not change that is no compliment. Human character and attitude are changeable.That means change is natural.

Our heart is larger than the sea. Our knowledge goes beyond universe. Yet weakness captures us. Narrow mindedness has become a natural trait.

Under these circumstances to be born as a human being is not an exalted state. It seems to be the lowest one. Even if one is born crying one should live a life filled with smiles. One should be instrumental in bringing happiness in the lives of others.

EVERYTHING IS WITHIN YOU

There is nothing which a man cannot achieve. With determination any impossible thing can become possible.

But one needs concentration. Only one work should be selected. If one thinks one can accomplish ten tasks at a time,ultimately one will succeed in none. It is an illusion to think that all jobs can be done by one person. Each one will become great depending on his capability and intelligence.

We should not waste our talents. We should have a goal. We should have a target. One has to work continuously to reach that target. Looking for short cuts and sideways is only an obstacle to victory. One cannot achieve what one wants, by shortcut.

Human power is greater than problems we confront. It we concentrate all our energies towards a single goal, any great work can be accomplished. It is natural to have problems. One should withstand them. We should prove the power of human existence.

The race horse has blinkers. It is to control its side glances. Then only it can run fast to reach the destination and be victorious. Similar is the case with us. We can achieve anything. But we have to control our wandering mind and get it to concentrate. Then there is nothing to challenge us.

Each victorious man has his past. Each defeated man has a future.

One has to be satisfied with insignificant results for insignificant work. On the contrary, if someone plans great and starts a great work, the result will also be great.

NO NEED TO REMEMBER

There are so many incidents in our life. We read so many things. We hear so many things. There is no compulsion that we should remember everything we see, read and hear. Infact, there is no need also. The anxiety to remember everything will spoil the brain. If we fill our mind with unnecessary things, where is the place for receiving new things? In this regard, forgetfulness is a boon. Without that there is no human existence.

There are many books in our library. Instead of having all those books in head, it is better to remember something good from the books to practise. That will make us happy but not remembering the books by rote.

In some context, we are not able to recall what we wanted to say. We feel sorry about this forgetfulness. This is not necessary.

If a thing is indeed important, the mind certainly registers it. If we are not able to recall something, it only means that it is not essential. So there is no meaning troubling oneself for not recalling the same.

We come across many in life. We make friends with some. With some others we have enmity for no reason. But the fun is we remember enemies more than we remember friends. It is unfortunate to remember the one whom we have to forget and to forget the one whom we have to remember.It is a good quality to forget the bad and to remember the good. Memory is a curse to person with vengeance. Forgetfulness is a boon to a person with forgiveness.

CAN BAD BE GREAT?

Suppose a person did not extend his help when we needed, we treat him as an enemy for lifetime. That enemity grows day by day.

He might have done an excellent job. Leave alone appreciating, we go out of our way to depict that as a bad work. We try to convince everyone we come across about that person with suitable examples and bombard them till they say we are right.

We exhibit broadmindedness in our words but we think in a narrow minded way. We follow narrow path and tell ourselves it is a broad way.

We may be good for nothing but when it comes to attacking the person we dislike our mind works brilliantly, we use all our energies to bring down the other person.

We forget the person who did good for us but remember the person who did us wrong and leave no stone unturned in taking revenge. But to long for someone else's downfall is a satanic pleasure devoid of human feeling. He may differ from us on a particular issue. He also has his opinion just as we have our own.

Without realising this we develop animosity and become victims of restlessness.

While there are many good deeds to do and responsibilities to shoulder concentrating on the single goal of bringing down our enemy is so ridiculous that even a vengeful cobra may laugh at it.

THOUGHT AND ACTION SHOULD BE THE SAME

There will be many problems if we start thinking everything should be according to our plan. To wish that way is mere selfishness.We always expect others to do the thing we want them to do. We can't tolerate even a little deviation.

But do we act according to other person's will? Can we do that? We don't care to think. Because for us, our own work is important. Each one has his own thinking. How can any person give shape to the thought that emanated from the other person? They may try to do what they have heard but how can they know at what level and in what form we thought about it? One can give shape to one's own thought. It is not possible for others.

When we are in a position to tell, we feel our importance. When we come to the position of being told, our opinion changes. Then we say, "He can say anything because it is easy. He does not know how difficult it is to accomplish. He thinks I am not doing it the right way. But can he do it himself?" Even the other person is the same as we are. We should be able to give a proper shape to our thought. We must be able to make it very clear to others. Then only others can do it the way we want it to be done.

Each one should shape his own thoughts. Shifting it to others means asking the other person to suckle our child and bring it up.

NOISE DOES NOT HELP

To talk less and to be more silent is good for us and our house. But we are more eager to talk than to work. We show great haste.

If we catch hold of someone, we don't leave the person. We don't even care whether they are listening or not, whether such a long talk is necessary or not. We continue our speech.

We don't care even if they are bored to death. We say whatever we wanted to say. Can we bear if the other person starts haranguing? No. Why? Because we think what we say is correct and what the other person says is not correct.

Under these circumstances, we become wild if the other person continues to argue. We try our level best to convince that man that he is wrong. This sort of argument only exhibits one's ignorance and it will never conclude.

There is no need for argument and magic of words if one has definite ideas.That person can do what he wants directly and accurately.When we don't have proper understanding, we are undecided and enter into an argument.As words flow, our shallowness too shows.When there is no matter, we gather wind.

It is an illusion to think that we can convince a person by talking a lot.

Silence itself is an answer for many words.

IT IS A WASTE NOT TO BE DIRECT

Unnecessary imitations, meaningless fears, many more misunderstandings always pursue us and trouble us. They make us hesitant. Besides certain beliefs become obstacles to our progress. We should overcome such obstacles. We should recognise the talent in the other person. Only those without values or talent take outward precautions. Do we give importance to the looks of Gandhi, Nehru or Tagore? We love the path they have chosen. We admire them. Worship them. We accept only their goodness and greatness.

Our life is our own. Our lifestyle is our own. But we need ideals of great people and the way they practised them. Experience is more important than letters, practice is more important than experience and the goodwill that comes out of that practice is of utmost importance. We should be careful not to find ourselves in an embarrassing situation.

Certain compromises may be necessary in a world where we do not understand ourselves. It does not mean we have to be submissive all the while. That is no life and there is no satisfaction in that. There are ways that help us to live as ourselves. But it takes time to reach our goals if we follow these paths.

The one who reaches his goal by foul means has to suffer mental and physical wounds. Can he then have the comfort of reaching his goal? No, he cannot.

If one works hard to reach one's goal the pleasure of reaching the same can be experienced. Let there be no show off or short cuts in our life. Let us proceed directly. Just because you are in a hurry, the cock does not crow and the day does not break.

ONE CANNOT SING IN ANGER

We are used to have some trouble or the other always. It has become natural for us to be morose, to crave for something or to get upset with meaningless thoughts.

A life which could have been happy is burdened with needless pain. We consider everything a problem. Even when things happen according to our expectation we are left with a little dissatisfaction.

If things do not happen the way we want them to happen, well, we feel that is the end of the world. There is a solution to every problem.Ultimately we will find it.

In the mean time we have endless anxiety. We are worried. We may hasten as much as we want yet each thing requires its own time. Since we cannot wait till then we get impatient.

At last we realise that all that agony was unrequired. We tend to think life is full of sorrow and we get a little happiness intermittently.

Whether it is a prince or a pauper he comes into this world crying. The beginning of birth should be the end of grief. The ultimate meaning of human life is to live happily. That is why whenever we are sad people tend to ask, "What is wrong? Why are you sad?" suggesting it is not natural to be sad.

When we are happy hardly anyone would ask, "Why are you happy?" That means happiness is natural trait of a human being.

We should spend a life filled with happiness realising that hardships come and go but happiness lasts in our life.

BRAIN IS NOT A DUSTBIN

We are curious to know everything. We want to know what is happening around us, about country's politics, about other countries in the world and about new development in ever growing field of science.

With this interest we accumulate as much knowledge as possible and share it with those around us. We express our ideas, opinions and discuss things with them. We gain new point of view. This way we enrich our knowledge.

It helps us to shape ourselves. If we confine ourselves to narrow point of view we get frivolous thoughts and get interested in insignificant things.

We get curious to know what this person or that person is doing. Our time is spent by criticising someone or by commenting on others deeds. We are all ears to listen to street gossip.

Are these the matters we are supposed to know? Should we use our intellect for this wasteful gossip? It should never be so. We have certain capability. We have some intelligence. If we canalise them in proper direction we will be in no way less than others.

We can make a niche of our own in society. We will be loved and respected. For this we have to harness our mind to be on the right path.

BE IN THE FRONT FOR A GOOD DEED

We certainly do a thing if we think that it is necessary and important. We may say," We don't have time at all," but we find time and get this thing done. If it is not important and not necessary from our point of view, we just cannot make it. We go on postponing. That work remains like that for ever.

If anyone asks us to do a favour, we will say, "Sure, I will do that." Later on, we analyse the pros and cons. "Will we gain anything out of it? Will that man be of any use to us?"

If we think there will be some gain, then we will give importance to that work. But if we think our labour, influence and work will go waste and the other person can be of no use to us, we will say, "Sorry" and leave it at that.

There is no complete truth in our words that it is not done because we are busy. If we are determined to do a thing, we will certainly find time and convenience.

We don't like a person who is of no use to us. If we think there is no benefit in doing the other person's work, we will be very busy.This kind of attitude should change. Anything that has useful result should be taken up and accomplished without any discrimination.

DON'T FEAR CHANGE

We want everything to work out in a systematic manner from the time we get up till we go to sleep again.

We start our day with prayer. We are careful not to miss our daily routine and exercise. We are also careful about food and sleep. We try to avoid coffee and tea. We are deadly afraid of habits like smoking. It is good that we are careful about everything in our life.

Since we are working within a frame with a fixed time schedule for everything, we are becoming our own prisoners. Life time is converted into an open jail.

We get upset when even one daily activity has missed from the routine. For example, if yoga is not done one day because of some urgent work, we feel sick the whole day.

Similarly, if we can't say our morning prayers for any reason, we think,"Today nothing is going according to plan.I am very upset. All this is because I missed my morning prayer."

This is an illusion. The weak thoughts are responsible for all these fears. In fact, our body is very strong and the heart is equally stout.

Rules and discipline are tools to give us comfort and peace. They themselves should not become our life. Anything that takes away our freedom does more harm than good.

FIND A SOLUTION THEN AND THERE

Seven deadly sins always follow a person. These evils harm the person as well as the society around. We don't treat addiction to card game seriously. When it comes to philandering we think it is confined to those who are involved in it.

We don't even object to people hunting dumb animals and eating their flesh because we don't have compassion.

Some are very angry by temperament. They abuse everyone. Since they don't care if one stays or leaves, the society absorbs them as well.

A lazy person who is greedy to rob others is also left untouched. Till he steals our money we are not bothered. The one addicted to alcohol suffers from ill health.

We think he is a burden to his own family, but does not affect us in any way. So we also don't take notice of an alcoholic person. Some people have this habit of blaming and abusing everyone. We forgive these people as long as they do not come anywhere near us.

We are least bothered when we have nothing to lose and no difficulty to face. This attitude has become part of our life. We think there is nothing greater than self-interest. We do not have courage to condemn the wrong.

Nor do we have guts to punish a crime. In fact a person's character is not confined to that individual and his family. An individual's act affects the society as well. A spark of fire can destroy the whole village but a single well can quench the thirst of all villagers.

KNOWN PERSON IS ALWAYS BETTER

Our strength depends on the number of relatives, friends and acquaintances we have. We need our people for good or bad in our life.

When it comes to practice, we are keeping all these people at a distance. We don't like to be employed with "our" people because we have ego that prevents us from asking for a job. Even if the job offer comes without our asking, then also we don't accept. Why? We don't want to be commanded. We feel our self respect will be offended. An outsider may insult us. It does not matter. If our own person shows a little anger, we cannot tolerate that.

Similarly when we are in a position to offer a job, we don't engage a person from our family circle. We fear that he will know all our secrets and will publicise them among other relatives.

We don't like to take a house portion for rent at a relative's place. We don't do business with them. We don't like even boundaries of properties with them, leave alone joint properties. We don't like to travel together.

This way we distance ourselves from our own people. Why should strangers who need not bother themselves with our troubles be concerned about our welfare?

Our own person benefits us in spite of differences. Only known relationships last long. It is mutually beneficial to be loyal to each other without feeling either superior or inferior.

IN LIFE OR DEATH HE IS YOUR OWN

We have many superstitions. Whatever suits our selfishness is the one we support as tradition. As long as a person is alive, we have great attachment and affection. We think we cannot live without him.

We have this tendency to think of good or bad at the time of birth as well as death.

How are we responsible for birth or death? It happens at a determined time. When we receive a card informing us about the death of a person, we immediately tear it off. We think it is bad to keep that card. This behaviour is limited to death ceremonies of others. If it is a case of our own, do we get the cards printed and then tear them off?

When a person is about to die, we bring him down to the ground. There is an unscientific belief that a person who dies on a cot has to face difficulties after life. So we make him lie on the ground.

It is all right to follow hygienic principles. But why is there so much hurry to send off a person? We can't die along with the person who is dead. So we shed copious tears and keep quiet. This is natural.

That body will leave his wealth, everything else behind and will soon be part of the earth. It is necessary to give send off to that person in a respectful way instead of making the body lie on the ground. It is shameful and inhuman.

These useless sentiments only reflect ignorance and are not symbols of the truth.

HERE AND NOW

When we have good fortune or face hardships, we attribute them to the good deeds of previous birth or fate. But we don't think that they are the results of good or bad we have done now. It is unnecessary to argue whether or not comforts and hardships are the results of the good or bad deeds we have done in our previous life. It is also unnecessary to know if things have fate.

We experience things which are the results of the deeds in this birth. We satisfy our present hunger by taking food now.We experience the difficulties which are the result of our negligence. We experience good results of our hard work.

We have results according to the good or the bad we do. The reasons for this experience are discernible in our deeds themselves.

Even if we do a bad deed thinking that no one is noticing, we are sure to experience its results one day or the other in one form or the other. There is a danger of losing faith in present deeds if we think of future births. It is clear that we get results of present deeds now itself.

A person leading a good life with a clean personality will reap good results in this life itself. There is no doubt about it.

If we get hurt now, we feel the pain now itself but not in the next birth. If we slip now, we fall now itself. When we drink water, our thirst is quenched. No injustice will be done to the good. Justice may be delayed but not denied. This is possible in this birth itself.

YOU DON'T BELONG TO YOURSELF ALONE

This is our life. It is our will. We know what is good and what is bad. We behave accordingly. We don't act according to the wishes of others. We are completely independent and free.

This is all very well. But you cannot say, "I will not do any work. I need not work. This is my will."

Lazy life is no life at all. In a hundred years life if the time spent in sleep is taken out, only fifty years remain. Of this one has to minus childhood and old age. Even diseases and discomforts have their toll.

Ultimately we have very little time for work. There is so much disenchantment. The feeling is, "However hard one may work, there seems to be no results. We are saddled with labour."

One should not always calculate in terms of gains and losses. Some results should be for us and some for society's benefit.

Whether we like it or not, we have to abide by a few principles.Life does not belong to us alone. Even to a **Sanyasi** who has given up everything, there is a fixed schedule. Don't we householders, and society have more responsibility?

Without entertaining lazy thoughts, we should continue to work. We will get result as our right.

CRITICISM IS NOT GREAT

When we sit together chatting, we feel very happy to talk about other people's bad deeds. We indulge in this for long without being tired. If we have to talk about some one's good, then we are really bored.

We don't care about a person who won an Oscar Award. If someone commits suicide because of personal hardships, we give a lot if importance to that and publicise. Good deeds and good news bore us. Bad news makes us happy, spirited and interested.

Good does not attract as much as bad does. We are very much interested to listen to bad things.We watch street fights and quarrels with interest.We are ready to show sympathy if someone is suffering. But if someone achieves something good, we don't go even a step forward to congratulate the person. We don't have a word. We don't discuss.

Not only that. We try to search for bad in good also. We don't take into account ninety nine good deeds done by the other person.If there is one mistake, we catch hold of that. Those who enjoy someone else's misery, can they withstand if they themselves are in the same plight?

We should not feel happy in fellow being's defeat. One can be human only when one appreciates the other person's greatness, accepts the good and emulates.

Bad spreads like wild fire.But it takes long for good to be evident.Bad gets publicised on its own.That is why good needs to be publicised.

IT IS FOR OUR CHILDREN ONLY

Marriage is a celebration. We don't have it again and again. This happiness is something which will not come back either for us or for our children. We put a false step in determining the level of celebrations. We are spending lavishly without a thought. "This is the first marriage in my family, my first son's marriage. So one should not think about expenditure. "So we go ahead and spend.

When it comes to girl's marriage, we say,"Only one girl. We should get a good alliance. Marriage should be celebrated on a grand scale." Then we go beyond our means and spend on dowry and marriage.

There is no end to spending if we go on adding, "How about this? Will not people laugh if this is not there?" There should be a limit to everything. There should be a plan. "Let us have this for the dignity. Let us save on this." Because of the money we spent in the name of children's marriage, all the hard-earned money which is intended to be useful to them, is wasted.

We should not rationalise that we are spending only on our children. Tomorrow, your children themselves may question, "Why did you spend so much on our marriage?" Celebration should leave sweet memories but not bitter experiences.

WE SHOULD CLEANSE OUR MIND

When it comes to habits we declare proudly, "I don't have any bad habits. I drink neither tea nor coffee. I can't stand cigarette smoke. I don't like those who drink." We even declare "I am a teetotaller."

It is good not to have bad habits and to be proud of it. But it is not good to look down on those with these habits, to humiliate them or to show contempt as if they need to be excommunicated.

Bad qualities are worse than bad habits. Habits will harm that one person or his family. But bad qualities destroy society, country and even the world.

One should give up bad habits that affect physical health. More than that we should also recognise the importance of mental health. The one who can declare, "I have no bad qualities" is the real hero.

One can live hundred years if one's physical health is good. But a person who is mentally ill tortures people around him.

Perfect health helps a person to live happily. But a complete person is useful to the whole society. Body is essential for individual and intellect for society.

A man is great when he can say, "I have no envy, no anger, no hatred. I have given up selfishness. I am free from the seven deadly sins." We salute him.

WE CAN'T BE ALL IN ALL

Can a person do all things at a time? The answer is 'no'. Because when we want one we have to lose the other. For everything we have to pay a price. When we think of our capabilities, resources and over and above time that is available in a practical way we know all these are limited.

To be a good husband one has to see that wife has no problems. One has to spend some time with the wife who is busy the whole day doing household chores. One should be of help to her. To be a good father one has to pay attention to children and lay foundations for their future.

While doing all these things, we should also see there are no shortcomings in performing our duty. We should be able to get work from those who are working under our supervision. We should not be temperamental.

We should be humble and obedient to impress those above us. We should not be negligent in our duty.

Then only we can achieve what we want and will be able to fulfil our desires as well as those of family members. Without giving up personal comfort we should enjoy life at every stage.

So it is necessary to accord priority to each task. Even if one thinks each task is equally important one has to have sequence in an intelligent manner.

If this is upset one has to face negative results.So our desires and responsibilities should be within our scope.

A person with such discretion and intelligence will be happy and will make others happy.

WE SHOULD NOT BE A MASS MEDIUM

We cannot keep to ourselves the things we know of others. If it is something bad, we just can't keep it. Unless we share it with others we suffer from stomach pain.

We don't give so much publicity if it is something good about others. We don't feel like sharing it with others. Moreover we feel irritated if others are praising that person. We don't like even to be at that place.

When we cannot help it we try our best to depict that person's good as bad. We try to convince others with bad jokes. If we succeed then our happiness knows no bounds.

Is it the thing we have to do as human beings? We should live up to the expectations of others that we can keep any secret, we are helpful to them as far as possible, and their secret is as safe with us as money in a bank.

Otherwise people hesitate even to talk to us. If we happen to enter when people are discussing something, on seeing us they stop their talk abruptly. They not only look down on us but also they try to avoid us as if we are untouchables. We get into this situation because of our tongue.

A human being should be an embodiment of trust. We should do the work that is entrusted to us properly. We should be able to keep others secrets. We should live up to the norm that no one is ruined because of trust.

EACH ACCORDING TO ITS LIMIT

We like a person means we take into account many of his traits which appeal to us. As long as we have good relations with them we don't notice their flaws. Suppose someone else criticises our friend we treat this person as our enemy. We even comment, "This fellow cannot recognise nobility."

As long as our needs and relations are there we praise the person to the sky high. If differences arise for any reason he suddenly becomes our enemy.

We try to degrade the same person whom we praised so much till now by heaping all his bad qualities on him thus dumping his reputation in the nether world.

There is no discretion here. We know that no person is complete or perfect. Why that far? Don't we have our own defects? Others are tolerating us, forgiving us and maintaining relations with us by taking into account only our good qualities.

Just because we have a well in our courtyard we are not drinking up the entire water. Just because there is plenty of food we don't gulp down all that is cooked. We eat only as much to satisfy our hunger.

We wear only one dress at a time but not all the dresses we have with us. That means we are living comfortably by limiting everything according to our need.

So also bonds, relations and human relations have to thrive within their limits.

YOU ARE WHAT YOU ARE

It is just not possiblc for us to be like someone else, or someone else to be like us. It is also not possible to mould someone else to be like one's own self. Each one will have his own style. If some are good at something, others are equally good at some other thing.

If we use our discretion and try to do the thing that is convenient for us and the one that we are capable of doing, we will get results that commensurate with our talent. What do we understand by this? That we need not compare ourselves with anyone else.

Even when it comes to gods, Brahma, Vishnu, Maheshwara too have different traits. All the three are performing three different types of duties. The first one is for creation, the second one is for existence, and the third one is for destruction. All the three are ruling three worlds.

It is appropriate for one to continue with the character in which he shines.Dividing people as high or low or wishing that everyone should live alike is against nature. Among us also some are peaceful by nature whereas some others are ferocious by nature.

It is good for one to maintain the character that is naturally accepted and recognised.

We can't search for strong emotion of Netaji in Gandhiji or peaceful nature of Mahatma in Subhas. There is no similarity between the two. Each one is different in form, character, behaviour and lifestyle.

You are what you are and that is real you.

WE SHOULD KNOW WHAT WE ARE DOING

Within our scope all of us are running a race for stretching our capabilities. Hard work is essential. So also getting results. But as we get results we become more ambitious. To reach that goal we work harder and life becomes tiring. We are not thinking even once why we are so anxiety-ridden.

We don't know why we are getting into more and more complex situations and for whom we are taking this trouble.

We may comfort ourselves saying, "It is all for myself, my happiness and comfort and for my wife and children." But it is not true.

There is no happiness in this anxiety-driven struggle. Nor can we please the wife and children. We are not able to do any good to society around since we ourselves are in turbulence.

Even when we achieve our goal with great effort, we see yet another goal before us. Again the same story. These desires and ambitions are changing into greed. In this endless struggle we remain dissatisfied. Let us not ruin our life like this. Let us live naturally in meaningful way.

If we are seeking only comfort and happiness is this kind of race necessary in life? Certainly not. After hard work there is need for rest. Whatever we may achieve that should give us comfort and happiness.

ONLY THINGS CAN BE DISTRIBUTED

When we have no problems, no difficulties we seem to be good people for all and all seem to be good to us. Only when we are in trouble and pain we feel like sharing it with others. We think of friends. Try to decide who is better.

It is a big question. We don't get sleep. We don't have mental peace. We think talking it over will help us. Then the telephone comes to mind.

Then we hesitate whether it is proper to call at that time. After debating with ourselves for a while we come to the conclusion that he can understand us. So we ring up.

"What's the matter, you called at this late hour" he asks. "Well, I was feeling very low. Felt like talking to you. Sorry, I troubled you," we apologise. "Oh no. It is all right. Tell me what is the matter?" the friend asks. We feel assured and explain things in detail.

"Don't worry. Everything will be all right" he says and listens to us. Yet his drawl, yawn come across. He may be cursing us in his heart of hearts thinking what a trouble at the midnight hour.

Yet outwardly he may encourage us to talk. So what we should realise is just as our comforts belong to us only, our problems are also limited to us.

When there is a thorn in your flesh others don't feel the pain. If there is light in your eyes it does not help others to see.

BLESS YOURSELF

We recognise that we should be doing well, be useful to others and for that we should be ever alert. Our theory is "Do or Die." Breathing courage we work hard day and night and achieve what we want. Thus we become famous.

There is no better moment of pride than to see our family members happy. We are overwhelmed with happiness when all others praise us.

Though we know that for doing anything we need an able body, we tend to neglect our health. We neglect because we think we can go to a doctor when something is wrong. We can buy medicines with money but not health. We can buy a comfortable bed but not good sleep. We can go on a pleasure trip but cannot be sure of happiness.

Though we know all these little things we tend to be indifferent. We are not giving at least half an hour to ourselves for physical and mental well-being and tranquillity. We consider it as a waste of time.

But this is a big crime we are committing against ourselves. We have to bear physical and mental pain all alone. No one can share it. Whether we say yes or no the body which is with us is totally depending on us. Whether we do good or bad that is experienced by body alone.

The body which will become one with earth is the one that is holding our life. The body that deteriorates alone can be our source of happiness.

Without self no one can do anything in this creation. Self is necessary for success and for treating others like one's own self.

DAY HAS AN END

We are busy with meaningless and purposeless tasks. If a work continues with commas, there is no peace. So there should be a full stop. That does not mean that we should lead a life without work.

We are living only to work. It is human law to work hard as long as one is alive. But our perpetual work should have satisfaction as its goal.

We can't work all the twenty four hours in a day. Having finished the day's work, one should have the satisfaction, "This result is enough for today."Having this satisfaction as foundation, the next day's work should start with enthusiasm.

Today's work should give us satisfaction but not dissatisfaction. If so, the next day's work will have dissatisfaction as its foundation. We cannot do any work properly amidst turbulence and agitation.

We get inpatient and intolerant. With these qualifications, no one can achieve anything.

Great deeds come out of peaceful mind. They have good results only. They give us comfort and make life happy.

A hard working person should have comfort and peace but no mental disturbance. For achievements, satisfaction should be the measuring scale.

FAITH SHOULD BE UNWAVERING

Many people have great belief in Vastu Shastra (the science of architecture). Some don't have any faith in this. There is no quarrel with them. Those who have faith in vastu should know that it is science.

Science does not change from person to person or house to house.

But some people with their half knowledge enter our home and without anybody asking, they give us innumerable suggestions making us feel breathless. They don't even give a thought whether we are in a position to do the alterations they suggested. We are left with deadly worry. We can neither follow their suggestions nor can we leave them aside.

We should not entertain these worries and fears. We need not believe everything the other person has said. If we have serious faith in vastu, then we should consult only one expert. We always think there is yet another person better than the one whom we consulted. We end up consulting a number of them. When the suggestions come from everyone of them, we find some of them quite contrary.

It leaves us quite undecided. Same is the case with fixing of auspicious time. Instead of the expected good, we are tying ourselves in knots.

We should get out of this fickle-mindedness. Any faith or any **shastra** should benefit us. It should not lead to chaos. Our fickle-mindedness alone is responsible for our difficulties. Infact, no shastra or no faith can frighten us.

DON'T FORGET TOMORROW

The moment we realize that our children are grown up and are of marriageable age our style changes. We start behaving in an artificial way. We start exhibiting a lot of goodness which has not been with us till then.

We have great expectations about money and dowry. But if anyone asks, "How much dowry are you expecting for your son" we dismiss it saying, "We are not bothered about dowry. We want the girl from a good family. She should be able to adjust well with us."

But it is not the girl, but the property she would bring that hogs our attention. Then why can't we go to a poor family in search of a suitable girl. No, we will never do that.

Someone or the other will be deceived by our words. The marriage will be fixed.Now we will show off our importance. Our anger, our superiority, our demands all start emerging during the marriage itself.

We may tell any number of lies for dowry. We torture the bride. We forget that we too have a daughter in the house when we subject bride's parents to various troubles.

First we say something, later we do something else. This is the greatest form of deceit. That is why whatever is said and agreed should be written on paper with the signatures of the concerned. Though it is not a legal document it can help in avoiding discord in the family.

Inspite of this if someone resorts to evil ways time will punish them. Till then forbearance alone can protect us.

ALL ARE POSSIBLE IF ACCEPTED

It is comfortable to rest on a soft silk bed. If one could sleep on it nothing like that. It is comfortable to get a variety of food prepared. To eat it is happiness. It is comfortable to own a car. It is happiness to drive in that. What we can buy is comfort and what we can experience is happiness.

We undergo a lot of hardships because we do not know the difference between comfort and happiness. Comfort depends on an outside factor. Irrespective of a thing or individual what one can experience is happiness.

One can be happy even if one is ill or one has no close relatives or one has no status. We are struggling, undergoing many difficulties, seeking favours from others in search of comfort thus subjecting ourselves to agony. In this process we are unable to understand a few realities.

We think it is comfortable not to work and laze about. We do not know that one who works hard gets happiness. We struggle to have an air-conditioned room, building and car. We don't so much desire as to have a full meal, sound sleep and freedom to go wherever we want. What does it mean? We are giving up those which give us happiness and are running after comfort. In this race we wear ourselves out and are miserable for not getting what we want.

We should accept those circumstances which we cannot change. We should have wisdom to know what can be changed and what cannot be changed. This wisdom comes from subtlety and truth is life's breath for subtlety. The life's breath is there in everyone. So it is everybody's right to be happy.

CONFUSION WITHOUT KNOWLEDGE

We don't know many things about ourselves, leave alone others. Our thoughts are not clear to ourselves. The day we know about ourselves and what we want, many of our problems will be solved. If not, every day we will be confronted with hardships.

The other person should respect us. He should have affection for us. Instead, we respect ourselves and love ourselves and call it self-respect grandiosely. When we are hurt, we talk of self-respect and self importance. This is indeed a climb down that we ourselves have to declare about our self-respect.

Almost everyone has a person above him. If he is humiliated there, he will resign the job. He is prepared to even beg for his livelihood instead of facing this humiliation.

Escaping is not the right action. He should face the situation courageously. He should have determination to win honour in the same place where he has been humiliated. If he leaves this place and goes elsewhere, there also he may have to face the same problem.

Human beings and their nature is the same everywhere. Circumstances do not change by changing places. Is begging not worse than the humiliation he has faced? Stretching the palm infront of everyone and facing their scorn does not enhance one's self respect or self importance. Self seeks peace, not respect. Peace comes out of good mind.

NOT BY WORDS-SHOW BY DEEDS

Generally, we have only one earning member in our families. All members are dependent on this person. We treat the earning member as head of the house. We respect him. The more he earns, the more happy we are.

We co-operate with that person to the maximum extent possible. He will be the centre of the house. We do everything with his permission. This earning member can be the husband, the wife or the child.

Husband brings home money and gives it to wife for expenses. If wife brings money, she gives it to husband and says, "As you please." If the child brings money, he will give it to parents.

All this is very well. But all the other members who are dependent on this person show their authority occasionally. We make him feel lonely.

Suppose he had been extravagant, or spent money for some fun, we don't keep quiet. We question him. "Why did you spend the money unnecessarily?"

Though he earned the money with hard labour, we deprive him of the right to spend. "You can only earn but should take our permission to spend," we say. What kind of justice is this?

It should never be hard work for some and authority for someone else.

YOUR THINKING AND THEIR ATTITUDE

We attend functions to meet others and to exchange pleasantries. Having gone there, we don't feel very free. In confusion we start chatting meaninglessly.

In fact our intention is to talk in a clever way to impress everyone. But that misfires. Then we feel it is better to get out of that place. Once out, we leave a sigh of relief.

Hypocrisy follows us without our knowledge. We fear others may take us lightly if we mingle freely. So we tend to be serious. Then we are criticised for our indifference.

We don't remember the names of some people. We know we have met them somewhere. We don't know what they are. In that case better to be frank and say we are unable to place them. It may be a little embarrassing in the beginning. Once we know who they are it is easy to carry on the conversation.

It is all right if we say "Sorry" for not recognising them. No one will find fault with us. Even if someone comments, "Yes indeed why should you remember us. You are a great person to notice people like us" we should not mind. Such people do not really care for us.

With some we are very close and with some others we are not. Sometimes not knowing what to talk we freeze and pretend to be serious. We should stop this deceit. We have what we have. Craving to have what we do not have leads to our mistakes.

Man is a free person. He becomes independent only when he behaves free.

GOOD FOR BAD

We have several small desires, little hopes and some tasks for accomplishment. To have them fulfilled, we sometimes seek someone's help. Either our friends or those interested in us help us in completing these tasks. We are grateful to those who helped us.

Some people have a tendency to help us and then to dominate us. They like to virtually ride on human beings. If we ask them, "Why are you commanding me so?" they will say, "Didn't I help you when you needed it?"

True, they helped. It is also just that we should do a good favour. But for one help, they can't seek ten favours from us. If we are in that position, it is all right. When we don't have that capacity, making demands and retorting "ungrateful fellow" indeed leaves us no where.

We have to repent why we sought his help at all. Mutual co-operation is the aim of social life. Showing authority beyond that, is unjust. If the person who got the help starts evading the person who helped him, it is a great wrong; equally wrong is the situation where the one who helped exploits the person who got the help.

Having done a good turn, one should forget about it. The person who received the help should remember it all through his life.

MONEY WITH FRAGRANCE

Once a fellow earned a lot of money selling milk. He put together all the money in a cloth bundle and was crossing a river. Then there was a big storm. His bundle got loosened. All the paper money flew off and only coins remained. He started crying that he lost all his money.

A sage who was passing this way asked the man what the matter was. This person replied,"My earnings from milk trade are lost in the river."

"Did you do your business honestly?"asked the sage. The businessman said,"Yes, Idid.""Are you sure that you didn't mix water with milk?" asked the sage.

The man confessed that he mixed water with the milk.

"Then why do you worry?" asked the sage. "The money you got by mixing water is mixed with the water now.The money you got out of milk is remaining with you in the form of coins. This money is the one which you earned justly. The money you got by unjust means vanished the way it came. At least now onwards, try to earn money by fair means. That will remain with you and give you comfort," advised the sage.

We don't understand the subtlety and try to earn as much as possible by all unfair means. This will only cause us misery. The hard-earned money by fair means is the only one that can give us happiness and comfort.

CIRCLE HAS NO DIRECTIONS

Why can't we be honest ?

Is it because of our weakness?

We have something in our heart. Our nature has something else. But we hide these to look different before others.

This may not be to cheat others or to keep them under illusion. In fact we may not have such bad thoughts or that kind of crookedness. It may be just to impress others.

Perhaps this is our undeveloped mind that prompted us to behave the way the others would like us to be.

If we think it is important that others should like us then we should develop those qualities instead of pretending to have them. That is not difficult but trying to impress everyone with our behaviour may be difficult to achieve.

Only the currency note printed by the Reserve Bank of India will be acceptable to all. No one else can claim to have that kind of acceptance. Even the laws which are applicable to all are also challenged. They appeal court after to court to get the judgment of their expectation.

Birth is ours. Death is ours. Man has to stand alone during most important facts of life. Then why should one crave for acceptance of others. Let us decide what is just in our own way.

In this world as an individual we should strive for our own individuality.

ALL OF US KNOW ALL THINGS

Just as we do certain things without a thought, so also we give advice unintentionally and mechanically. We don't care to know whether the other person is in a condition to receive our advice or not.

Is there anything that is freely available in this world? The answer is, "Yes, advice." Those who seek advice do so only to hear what they themselves would like to hear.

Even before the other person narrates his problem we are ready with advice because we want to be counted among his well wishers.

In addition we also want the other person know that we have a good opinion of him. Sometimes there is this cunning that without giving anything we want to extract from him the thing we want.

We intrude into their lives by commenting on their habits, lifestyle, their income and expenditure, the way they bring up their children, their education, employment and you name it we are ready with our comment.

If someone approaches us for our opinion or for a solution they themselves could not find, or for some information they urgently need, our sincere advice may help them.

But casual talk or "free advice" is meaningless. Let advice be in a little measure but it should be useful.

There may be many people who can advice. But two helping hands are always more useful than mere advice.

LOVE AND BE LOVED

We have many problems. We are afraid to tackle them. This is our inability to find a solution. So we cheat ourselves. We move about happily with self-deceit. We pretend as if everything is fine.

If anyone asks. "Why are you like this? Why don't you talk to people? Why don't you socialise? Why can't you laugh heartily?" we brag, "Well, I don't like such frivolities. I have my own individuality. I can't be servile. There is no need for that."

Though we know in our heart of hearts these are all signs of our incapability, we snuff out our own conscience and tell ourselves, "It is true I have a lot of self-respect. I cannot stretch my hand before anyone. I don't take help from anyone."

By thinking no one is good and thus distancing oneself from everyone, deprived of love we are becoming sadists. Love and hatred are natural for everyone. The one who gives up hatred alone can cultivate love and affection.

If one says, "I will not ask, I will not allow others to ask" it only means he neither gives nor he cares. If one says, "I will not abuse, nor will I be abused," it means he neither loves nor will he be loved. If one says, "No one can point a finger at me" it means there is no friendly hand that is reaching to him.

The one who is aloof becomes a burden to society, family and to his own self. The one who sits on the bank is useful to none. The one who gets into water alone can be victor or conqueror of death.

IT IS NOT THE THING BUT THE UTILITY THAT MATTERS

The most certain address of ours is telephone. This is where we are caught by anyone at anytime. We face many tricky situations because of the phone. We may be working with great concentration. There the telephone rings. We pickup the phone and listen to some news. That disturbs our mind. The work we are doing is also spoiled.

If the telephone rings at the midnight or at any odd time, there is no way we can leave it unattended. When we pickup the phone it may be an important matter or wrong number.

Because of the telephone, we hear harsh things for no reason."The other day,I rang up four times.They said you were not at home," the other person will say finding fault with us.

What purpose will be served by ringing up even ten times when we are not there? Without understanding this, why does he think that we have done something wrong?

Some, who do not like us particularly, ring up, hurl abuses without mentioning their name. Others bother us with unnecessary matters.

Under these circumstances, we convey the message we are not available. Then we feel sorry that we have told them lies. What to do? It can't be helped. Otherwise the man would take life out of us with his lengthy talk.

So the telephonic conversation should be brief, to the point and frank.This is beneficial to both sides.

The instruments which came into existence because of brain power of human beings should be helpful aids but not commanding masters.

FOOD IS NOT FOR EXHIBITION

When we celebrate a marriage or house warming, we take many precautions. We want to serve good food on the occasion.We get a lot of dishes prepared. We take extreme care in their number, taste and hygiene. We welcome the guests warmly and serve them all the dishes. But we don't give our guests opportunity to enjoy the food leisurely.We don't serve them leisurely. We think our duty is over by serving all items together.

Since many others are waiting,we want the present batch to finish their food fast. This way we are only exhibiting a number of things before them but not giving them an opportunity to enjoy the food.

Many people cannot withstand this rat race and taste a bit and finish their meal. Some others are not eating at all. There are yet others who think that an invitation to food means an invitation to starving. Many take food in the feast and then go home and have their own meal.

It is not important how many people we invited and how many types of food we served. It does not matter if there are not many invitees. It does not matter if there are not many dishes. These are immaterial. The most important thing is, the guests should have their food with satisfaction. A guest should not be made to think, "Instead of this food, it is better to have my own Spartan meal at home."

Any task should have the same amount of concentration in the beginning, the middle and the end.

HEART IS THE HOME OF JOY

We feel happy when our friend, a person with whom we moved closely achieves something. We congratulate him. Yet in our heart of hearts there is envy troubling us.

Why am I not able to grow like him is the nagging question. We are disappointed thinking that in spite of our best efforts we are getting no results whereas the other fellow has all the luck.

This kind of feelings and thoughts cause restlessness. As a result we become weak and depressed. We will not be in a position to do even things which we are capable of doing.

The people around us are also responsible for developing this kind of jealousy. They compare us with others. "Why can't you achieve the same?" they ask. They make fun of our intelligence and effort.

What we need at that time is inner strength. We should not care for the comments of these ignorant people who hurt us with their words.

If we observe we know that we are not envious of everybody in this world. That is why we hero worship those strangers who achieve so many things. We also want to be like them. That is why we get inspiration from Bill Gates, the Tatas and the Birlas.

It is not in our nature to be envious. This is an intermittent bad thought. If we are envious by nature we should be unhappy about everyone who is better than us. But we don't do that. Independent thoughts like "This is my life and this is my own," will uplift us.

WE ARE PAINED MEANS WE PAINED OTHERS

Among us everyone is an incarnation of love. We have an ocean of love within our heart. Yet all of us lament and complain, "Oh, there is none to love me."

Because we are not trying to know who is loving us. Even if we knew we take him for granted and do not care for him.

As a result that person undergoes mental agony and thinks love is a crime. In fact love is like a chain. If a person loves us we love some other person.

This other person loves yet another person. Without realising that a person who loves is with us, just behind us, we look to the person before us and crave for his love.

The same wounds which we inflicted on others are being inflicted on us by some other people. Thus every one is losing mental peace and suffering from loneliness.

Instead we should try to know who loves us the most and return that love so that there will be mutual loving leading to a loving life.

All have attachments and affections. But they are all misplaced. Though this process seems to be connecting it leaves everyone alone. It is necessary to look back in love instead of looking ahead.

Because in this forward looking attitude love becomes blind. When we look back the eyes of love are open wide.

WORRYING IS HARMFUL

We have some problems and we go out of our way to get some more problems. Anyway the whole life is spent with some problem or the other.

While doing a work we need concentration, diligence and suitable preparation. Once the work is over there is no need to think about the same.

If in the middle of the work we think of something else and try to do that way the first plan will be gone. Then we can't implement the second one also. Ultimately the outcome will be substandard.

Why should it happen this way? Because we are anxious to do every job perfectly. That is where we are mistaken. What are the criteria for perfection? What is the yardstick?

"Perfection" is something which everyone decides for oneself. What is "perfect" to someone may not be perfect for others. No work will have all inclusive complete form.

It is enough if we try to be better than others around us. Any effort towards this is good. When compared with another if our work comes out better that is enough. We should treat this as yardstick.

We should not worry too much thinking about perfection and completeness. Our own delineation of perfection should not make us the prisoners of the same. Every work that can be done should be done according to a plan. There is no point regretting later.

The arrow that has left the bow will not come back. The word that is uttered cannot be taken back. Having done a work one should not go back to it. Whatever we can do, that is our notion of perfection.

GIVE SUPPORT TO A CREEPER

We are not doing everything at the right time. Discerning good or bad, being just, righteous, doing the right thing and giving up the bad thing should be adopted while one is young.

When everything is over and we are about to leave the world, we think of the **Bhagavad Gita.** We weigh good or bad deeds. We attend spiritual gatherings.

What do we do knowing all these things in the old age? In that state when we are in no position to do any good, what is the use of this knowledge? What can we do and show to anybody when we ourselves are mentally and physically depending on others?

In these spiritual gatherings, they tell us how to be courageous while confronting difficulties. Infact everyone of the audience is an experienced one who has seen many ups and downs and is in a position to tell how he faced difficulties in life and solved the problems. So what purpose will these speeches serve? Nothing.

This kind of philosophy is for the young. They are the people who should know. When they put it into practice, they will be better off and also better the society.

So all these forums should concentrate on them. Spiritual teachings should be attractive to the youth. Then only the individual and the system will get benefitted.

NIGHT IS THE FUEL OF THE DAY

Sleep is a great boon.It is the one and only means to forget hardships, pains, griefs, in short the whole world.

Perhaps that is the reason why in the creation day and night are there. Except human beings, all other creatures enjoy nights.

But for us, it is work-endless work and thoughts related to work. This unceasing anxiety does not allow us to have the comfort of sleep.We take pills to induce sleep.We consume alcohol. We meditate, read books, watch movies and we virtually do penance for sleep. But do we get sleep? No.

That is why sometimes we dread night."Oh, my ! should I spend a sleepless night today also?" is our fear. All others in our neighbourhood are sleeping. Only we are wide awake like nocturnal spirits. We don't know what to do.

With money, one can have an airconditioned bed room. There could be an expensive double bed. Yet there is no guarantee for sleep. Sleep is something which one can neither buy nor borrow.For this comfortable, natural sleep one should give up those tasks which deprive one of the sleep. Unending thoughts and works should be confined to evening.Then sleep will welcome us the same night.

EACH MOMENT IS GREAT

Human life, especially healthy active life, is short. Even this short span of life is wasted in unnecessary obstructions created by us. Faith in a few things is all right but to consider good or bad before each task is becoming too much with us.

We have too many superstitions with regard to a favourable day, favourable star and favourable time. We don't start anything, we don't go anywhere if time is not auspicious. We are not able to understand how these superstitions are torturing us and how they are wasting our valuable time.

Good or bad is related to human nature but not to time that belongs to nature.

Infact in twenty-four hours, each hour and each minute is valuable. They do us good only, not harm. If not, how will the nature operate? How do sunrise, sunset and moon rise happen at a particular time without taking into account auspicious time. In a year, all three hundred and sixty five days are good. We survive if only we breathe every minute and every second.

Suppose we stop breathing thinking that it is not auspicious time, we will drop dead in no time. So every moment that is keeping us alive, is great.

DO IT NOW, NOT LATER

We don't realise the value of a person when he is alive. When that person is away from us or when we lose that person, our affection overflows. We recall his goodness, his qualities and express our sorrow.

If we could express even a fraction of this love when he was alive, how happy he would have been. But we don't give him that opportunity to be happy.

When a writer, an artist or a great man dies we say, "A Star is gone"and "A great man passed away leaving a void which can never be filled." We deliver speeches, organise condolence meetings, publish enlarged photographs and to perpetrate his work, we establish memorials. Then we feel we have done a lot of social service. But when they are alive, we don't care to know how they are living, what hardships they are facing, and how disappointed they are that their work has not seen the light of the day.

We should give them our helping hand while they are alive. If we help a person by informing the people about his great work, the amount of pleasure and encouragement an artist will get is enormous. With that inspiration he works more in creative field which will reach the society. It is good to remember and to express sorrow. It is a duty as well. But if we don't care for a person when he is alive and have meetings organised later, they serve no purpose.

It is not very important to have prayer meetings for the peace of the departed soul. To have a kind heart that will make a living person happy is more important.

EVEN IN DREAM WE LOSE SOME

By nature we are selfish. "My welfare is very important to me" is the thinking. Before undertaking any work we contemplate, "Is it beneficial to me?" We give importance only to personal interests.

Even that we don't do with dedication and efficiency. We just dream big and never think about the effort involved.

We know we can be elevated by working honestly in the present job. Yet we neglect our work. Knowing that conducting business wisely and justly will lead to our development we tend to choose unfair means.

Even when a doctor advises us to follow certain diet and discipline for our own good we don't listen. This way we are rebelling against ourselves. We are becoming our own enemies. We are losing control, courting disaster only to regret later.

One thing becomes clear. Even selfishness needs a little sacrifice. When we want one we have to give up another. Our tendency is to have everything we desire without giving up anything.

We have to work hard even if it is for our own selves. We should be able to give up certain things. Then only a person can develop. When individuals develop the society develops and common good is achieved.

START SLOWLY

We are eager to have near contacts. It is good if these contacts grow systematically.But we are anxious to get closer. In this haste, we cross our limits. We exhibit a lot of love showing many courtesies. If the other person is travelling, we go up to the railway station to see him off.

The moment the other person reaches his destination, we telephone him and ask, "Have you reached safe? Did you have a comfortable journey? Could you sleep last night in the train?" Oh, we put several questions and try to please the other person as much as possible.

When we do all these things,the other person is pleased. "Ah, what a friend I have!" he says to himself. It is all right. But can we extend these courtesies everytime? No. Because we have our own work and own problems.

When we are entangled thus, if this person visits us,we may not be in a position to show these courtesies. Then what will he think?

"Why did this man change so much? He does not have the same respect or love for me."He will be hurt and unhappy.

Same is the case with us. When he goes away we start regretting,"I could not even talk to him properly.What would he have thought of me?". Had we been in our limits in the beginning itself, we would not have faced this situation. We ourselves should help this world in understanding us.

INTROSPECTION IS NEEDED

We can't be steady even for a while.Mind wanders and the body does not stay at a place. With this, we are always in a hurry.

For example, we set out for the Lord's darshan in haste. If someone goes before us, we start fighting. We don't think peacefully that we also will get our turn. We are selfish to think that God belongs to us only.

Should we think all this is our devotion to God? Very doubtful because there are a few special poojas to the Lord. Then one can sit peacefully for half an hour to one hour in front of the Lord. If we get such an opportunity, do we continue to see the Lord and think of Him? No.

We look at the person sitting by our side. Then we look around to see what others are doing. If we get an opportunity, we indulge in murmurs. If not, we become sleepy and may be we go to sleep.

We are so great that even if God manifests Himself and stays a long time with us, we get bored. "Why is he staying with us for so long? I wish He could vanish! We have already told Him what we want. It is better he gets out and attends to work."

In life, we always try to reach out for something. Once we get it, we become disinterested. We can lead happy life when we start enjoying the present, invite the future and make it comfortable.

TELESCOPE FOR THE SKY, NOT FOR THE HEART

We expect result for every work. We don't take up any work if it is not gainful. We cannot withstand if anything goes wrong.

That is why we are very much interested to know what the future holds for us. We search out means to know our future. We depend on palmistry, numerology, astrology and other things.

Science has progressed so much but there is no science which can tell about man's future. Our ancient treatises are also not completely dependable. All these are theories based on faith.

When we have faith a few things may come true, a few things may not come true. When the results are convenient we think ancient references are great. When things are not convenient we think otherwise. All these are accidental matters. There is no such great wonder that would happen in human life without effort.

We can have mental peace only when we put an end to such fantasies.Then we are clear about things we have to do. When we do what is to be done results come on their own. No eyes can read what is destined. That is why people call it Brahma's script.

It is said that Brahma Himself forgets what he has written. If so how can we people grasp it. All this is a mere illusion. Whatever destined will certainly happen. No power can obstruct it. Then why do we discuss these matters if not to lose our mental peace? We should accept whatever comes our way. A person who moves ahead without getting into the complications of astrology alone can achieve success.

IT IS EASY TO BE GOOD

We often think, "There is no place for good and there are no good people in the world. We do not know whom to trust. "In fact, the world is not that barren. Unlike riches that belong to a few, goodness is not confined to a few only.

Goodness is not anybody's monopoly. It is spread world wide. It is there in everyone to certain extent. It is quite possible what we like may not be liked by others and what others like may not be of our liking.

This should not make us think that the other person is wrong and we are right.

Some how our thinking begins with the suspicion, " The other person may not be a good person."

If our outlook is not good, the feeling that all others are bad gets strengthened. In fact it is bad to think that we alone are good.

We need not make any special effort to live as good people, to have good thoughts, to do good deeds and to be called a good person. Our goodness within is frozen.

We have to thwart it.When the water is frozen it becomes ice. If we add water to it, the ice melts and we get cool drinking water.

If we open the doors of good within, good winds will blow in. They purify us and cover us with goodness. It is very difficult to be bad. It is easy for all of us to be good.

ONE PEN AND MANY WRITINGS

As we grow old we lose our mental faculties. Body does not cooperate. Many ailments surround us. No energy is left for any work. We know all this. More important is our inability to shed tears when we are faced with difficulties.

As one grows old mind becomes hard. Grief is frozen. It does not come out. It fills the heart making it heavy. So we don't even have the relief of shedding tears.

Look at the children. They cry for every small thing. The very next moment they start laughing. We are not understanding how great a boon this one is. Children as they cry, so they laugh the moment they get what they want.

As we grow old we lose sensitivity. Grief is gulped down. Faced with problems we undergo mental agony. In the process our mind and body grow rough.

We call this roughness euphemistically maturity. We do not realise that the heart stopped responding and mind lost its vibration.

So we should experience every moment. We should not suppress feelings thinking it is wrong to weep and ridiculous to laugh. One should laugh whole heartedly.

Faced with grief one should weep to heart's content. This cleanses body of all unclean matters, frees one from diseases and relaxes nerves.

If one can preserve childhood even in old age man can be happy for ever.

DON'T BE UNGRATEFUL

The best quality one can possess is to do good for others. The one defect a human being has is not to have gratitude. Those who are caught in difficulties, finding no way to overcome them, cannot do so without somebody's help.

Under such circumstances sometimes even friends and relatives do not come forward to support them.

It is said that as you sow, so you reap. It seems it is not applicable to human beings. We are forgetting our minimal duty of being grateful to those who helped us.

For every little assistance and cooperation we utter "Thank you" from the tip of our tongue. We do not have the good sense to recognise the good that is done to us.

Poison can never acquire the quality of milk. Milk has nothing to do with the evil in poison. But we are the type who forget the milk we drank.

Though we do not remember those who helped us, we very well remember those who did a little harm to us at any point of time.Let them be punished, we think. We don't keep quiet with that. We vow that we will take revenge. Why this meanness?

We should not yield to darkness like new moon night. We should be like the sun spreading light and welcoming auspicious mornings into life.

RESPONSIBILITY AND SELF-RESPECT

We forget that we are all bound by time and age. As long as we are active we don't care for anything. We go overboard for wife and children.

When we get old children are not willing to shoulder their responsibilities. When we are powerful everyone is respectful. Outwardly they pretend to love us.

Just a look from us and they would have done what we wanted. So we are thrilled forgetting hard times are ahead. If we can attend to our own things with a little effort, other members of the family can do a little more for us.

It is said that while earning one may earn as if one is living forever, but when one gives away in old age one has to give as if the end is tomorrow.

When we visit someone it is better to return the same day even though they implore us to stay for a day more because anyway the next day we have to leave.While advising the young it is better to be brief while they pay attention. If we prolong it they feel bored.

It is somewhat better not to depend economically on others. So we have to invest for ourselves. Not that we cannot trust our children. This is only to improve our self-confidence.

Thus when we act with foresight there is no need to depend on others. We can as well sit back and relax.

THERE IS A DIFFERENCE BETWEEN A HAND AND ANOTHER HAND

The strange thing is we have many wants when we don't have money. "I would like to buy that or this. Let me eat this. I should go to that town. I like to wear those clothes.I want to have outings." There is no end to these desires.With this, we waste what little money we have.

If we are still not satisfied, we borrow money and later face hardships. Then we will come to a state when we have to borrow from several people. This is one type of story.

Suppose we have earned the money,our mind changes. We don't spend even a single rupee on ourselves. We don't like to help others.We don't spend on clothes, food or outing. This is another type of story.

If a rich person becomes stingy and does not spend even a paisa, it is said that Goddess of wealth Lakshmi feels hurt thinking,"Why is this fellow imprisoning me who is meant to be of use to others."

Similarly if a person spends beyond his means, then also Lakshmi feels sorry.

"Why is this fellow not being careful? Why is he losing me thus? How will he meet his future needs if he is impoverished?" So she will leave both types.

If a rich man does not spend reasonably and if an ordinary man spends beyond his means, both are at fault. Each one should do what he is supposed to do.

WE ARE MODELS TO OUR FAMILY MEMBERS

Generally it is said a house will indicate what type of a person the housewife is. Infact, it is right to say children of a house indicate what type of persons the husband and wife are. If we are fond of things, we keep house neat. If we compete with our neighbour, then we can decorate our house better. But these are not important.

The important thing is to take care of our children. We should mould their behaviour. We should pay attention to their education. But we are neglecting this area. Because we love our children excessively, we don't find fault with them anywhere.

We don't chide even when they misbehave with the guests. When they fight with the neighbours' children, we always support our children. When they insist on buying something, we don't mind. This sort of bringing up will only spoil our children.

We boast, "We have a dining table, T.V.and fridge." Infact, we should be proud to say, "Our children are good at studies.They listen to us.They respect elders." We give importance to outer beauties and neglect inner beauty.

We should be fond of children's deeds and not children themselves. Never mind how the house looks, it is a must that people in the house should be all right.The world should appreciate our attitudes,instead of the things we have accumulated.

YOU CAN TAKE ONLY WHEN YOU GIVE

We don't do even an iota of work without expecting something. Our prayers, worship and all other things are performed with some expectation.

If we have a problem God should come immediately to sort it out. He should grant our desires in a moment. If He delays this action or if we don't get what we want we don't keep quiet. We sulk.

We bombard Him with arguments. "We worshipped you in so many ways. Had special prayers. We offered many gifts. What did you do in return? Why don't you solve our problem? Why don't you give us what we want?"

When it comes to human relations we adopt a different method. We promise to get something done and take the remuneration beforehand. We promise we complete a particular job by a particular time.

We also discuss and agree on terms and conditions. But the work to be done is postponed without fail. But in the case of God it is not so. We don't want it to be so. We think He has no other work except attending to all our problems.

But God belongs to all. All are His children. He knows better what is good and what is not good for us. If we free ourselves from worry He on His own will grant what we need. He leaves out things which are not necessary. There is no need to remind Him of His duty. If we do our work properly we will certainly get results accordingly.

DIFFERENT JOURNEYS

Whenever we get an invitation from those who love us and care for us we should accept it. We should take part in their celebrations, share their happiness and wish them well.

Suppose we can't make it to the occasion, we should meet them later, explain the situation and continue to have good relations.

Even if we cannot visit them for a happy occasion, we should certainly meet them when something unfortunate happens. No reason is big enough to stop us from visiting them. We should meet them irrespective of how good or how bad our relations are with them.

We should console them and share their grief. We should give them courage. We should support them by word and deed.

Instead of doing that we engage ourselves in conversation with others. We form into groups. At one place it is politics. At another place business is discussed. At some other place comments on neighbours continue.

In fact there the talk should be on the departed person, about his personality, his greatness and things we can learn from him. When we are engaged in gossip the whole purpose is lost.

When a lamp is in a temple we express our devotion. If it is in a liquor shop we light a cigarette. Though the lamp is same its value changes according to its place. So our behaviour should be appropriate to the context.

We attend a marriage only when we are invited. But in the case of death we need no invitation.

ACCEPT WHAT YOU HAVE

We request others especially seniors not to be cross with us on a festival day.

We request our friends not to make fun of us and not to hurt us on that day.

But at home we are annoyed with the house wife. We complain that food is not cooked well or house is not kept neatly or children are not disciplined duly.

Then she tells persuasively, "Won't you stop criticising atleast on the festival day.Forget the problems and be happy. When you are at peace the whole household is happy with celebrations."

Till then we don't realise that we expect something and we ourselves follow a different thing. We don't give up our bad habits even on that day. We don't stay at time to spend some time with the family. We go out wandering in the street aimlessly or indulge in gossip wasting time.

We should realise the importance of a festival and celebrate it accordingly. All our festivals are unique and variant. Each festival has a meaning and purpose.

When we celebrate a festival according to the tradition it becomes a real festival.

As soon as we wake up we pray that this festival should be good to us and should bring happiness through out the year. But we don't tell ourselves, "Today I won't commit any mistake, I won't accuse anyone, I won't blame anyone, and I won't hate any one." Only good thoughts lead to good results.

EACH BIRD BELONGS TO ITS NEST

We tend to underestimate everyone. We make fun of the other person saying, "What does he know?" There is a great surgeon. He may not know how to thread a needle. There is a great scholar. He may not know how to swim. How can we estimate the other person's standard with our thinking? Each one has his own knowledge. It is wrong to compare one with the other and then underestimate others.

This is all because of envy which does not allow us to accept the other man's greatness. If there is no talent, how can a person become great? Because they have command over their own fields, they are famous. We think, "I have read so much. I learnt so much. This one who does not know a thing is getting a great name in the society." But surely, he would have had his own scholarship.

If we don't have essential knowledge and acquire some other knowledge, what purpose will it serve?

It is ridiculous to ask a successful farmer, "Who won Nobel prize for literature this year?" and make fun of a writer, "You don't even know how many cents to an acre. What sort of writer are you?"

If we underestimate the other person because he does not know that we know, it only shows our shallowness. It does not anyway diminish the other person's talent.

HARDSHIPS DO NOT STAY FOR EVER

Each one has his own difficulties. There is no exception here. But we think that only we have difficulties and others are happy. If any one says, "Why are you so worried for such a small matter?" we retort, "You can say that being furtunate as you are. We have our problems." We don't think that even the other person has his problems and botherations.

We sit near the ocean for mental peace. We look at the sea but don't understand the agitation the sea is undergoing. The sea which is occupying three thirds of the earth too has its ebbs and tides. This earth on which we are standing steady is also revolving around the sun. Each one has a gulf within. There are many things which cannot be expressed.

We cannot find solutions to our problems but we have solutions for the problems of others.

The other person's problem is small and can be easily solved. If it comes to us, oh, the most difficult problem confronts us.We also think,"He does not know a thing. So he is not able to resolve his problems."

Moreover, we have this arrogance that we are very intelligent and can find a solution to any complicated problem. Each one has to solve one's own problem. We should limit ourselves to rendering a little help and advice. The others can resolve their problems on their own.

THINK BEFORE YOU ASK

We approach others for help when we can't do a work ourselves. We request them, "Please do this for me and help me overcome my difficulties."

The other person has sympathy for us. Yet he may say, "I have to request someone else for this. Imagine how delicate I feel about it. So I can't help you."

Every person has someone above and someone below. There are people who seek our help and we seek some other's help.

We also don't help everyone the moment they ask for help. We think perhaps our influence may be lessened if we start helping everyone. Perhaps it is true. However important a person may be, he can help only within certain limitations.We should realise this truth.

Before seeking favour from others we should ask ourselves whether we will do the favour if we are in their place. If we start spending money wastefully just because we have it, one day we will be left with nothing.

If we misuse power we lose honour and prestige. It is not only money even influence should be utilised with care.

It is not proper to ask for everything with a light attitude it is all right whether he does it or not. One should ask only when there is no other go.

The other person should feel sorry if he does not do the work instead of we feeling bad about it. That means our need should be so true and accurate.

MENTAL PEACE IS IN THE MIND ITSELF

Why do we want success in life? With the hope we get peace and happiness. But when we reach the desired goal we are still left feeling restless. Does it mean one will have mental peace in defeat? No. That is still more horrible.

When we achieve what we wanted to achieve one thing comes to our mind. "There are many who do not have money and position as much as I have. Yet they are all happy and comfortable. Only I have to slog like this without proper food or sleep."

But then, who forced us to occupy that elevated seat and to achieve success? We do it driven by great ambition to have fame, name and money and to be rated as far superior to others.

It is not an ordinary thing to better one's own position and also to help others. This tendency is worth emulating.But after all the achievement if we start complaining, "There is no happiness in this" others are baffled.

To achieve something we have to give up something. What we have now is the one which we desired once. We yearned for it and achieved it.

Are we enjoying this with the same intensity as we longed for it? In spite of the achievement we are restless and dissatisfied only means there is something wrong with our thinking.

When we really respect and value our achievement we certainly get peace and happiness.

The concerted effort we put in with a satisfied mind alone can help us climb higher and higher. Just as we are responsible for our victory, we are also responsible for our peace and happiness.

WE HAVE TO LOOK UP TO SEE THE PEAK

We hesitate to talk to people in high places. We compare ourselves with them and think we cannot be any where near them. We should certainly respect elders. But there is no need to fear them. It also does not mean we should be callous in our behaviour.

Many a time we think we are inferior to others and hate them for that. We tell ourselves, "Let him be great. How does it matter?" If the other person is in a position we say, "How long will that last?"

If it is about moneyed person we please ourselves abusing him, "What show off! Had not we seen rich people like this before? Didn't we see them fall flat? This fellow thinks his riches will last for ever."

In fact those people have nothing to with our thoughts. All these troubles are due to our feeling that we are inferior to others. This restlessness is because of our low self-esteem.

The restless mind troubles us. So we try to project ourselves as great people. We boast saying, "We have our individuality. We don't yield to materialistic needs."

All this is a big lie. If not for materialistic things, are we living for salvation through spiritual contemplation? Bunkum. Every one works for his own benefit. Leave alone money, no one is prepared to give even physical help for a fellow human being.

Then why this hypocrisy? The positive attitude of accepting the other person's greatness will help us in ourselves becoming great.

IS NOT EYE IMPORTANT ?

We should agree that every person is selfish. He thinks about his interests and is self-centred. It sounds grand when one says, "For me every one is same. All are equal. I don't differentiate between people." But hardly we come across people who practise this.

Well, when we leave aside exceptions, generally we consider those who think of our well-being as our well wishers.

It is important to pay attention to priorities in life. There is nothing wrong in it. While we are talking on the phone if we get another important call, it is all right to tell the first person, "I call you later" and hang up to receive the important call. There is no arrogance here.

The first person need not think we neglected him. Similarly among friends, acquaintances and relatives it is necessary to greet first those who are close to us. When it is their turn they also do the same.

In this process it is meaningless to think someone is neglected or humiliated. Even while performing our duty we follow the same method. So we organise our tasks according to priority.

Suppose we mix up this order, get confused or undecided what to do first we don't get results. Only by being frank we can recognise those who are close to us and those who are not so close to us.

WE WILL BE CAUGHT WITH OUR STRATEGIES

In order to please others we start exchanging pleasantries. "Hello, how are you? How is your wife? How are children? What are they doing? It is a long time since we met."

After all this we are bound to ask them the favour we wanted. It may not be our intention to cheat them or deceive them to get our work done. All we want is to see that they are in a good mood before we talk to them about our work.

If we are sincere in our approach in asking the other person about his welfare our love and affection touch their heart. There is nothing wrong in talking pleasantly. It is necessary to have some introduction.

It is not proper to ask straight away "Will you do it for me or not?" One should not presume that no one can say "no" to his request.

The problem is in talking in a round about way or in scheming to get work done by showering praise. This will give negative result. Once our secret is out we won't be able to face them again.

If we are clear about the kind of help we need the work will be done easily. Or atleast it is known that we are not of dual nature. Direct approach and subtlety in thinking will yield good results.

THERE IS A DIFFERENCE IN PROCESSIONS

We commit some mistakes knowingly, and some unknowingly. It is all right if we ourselves bear the results but on many occasions they bother others.

We can play tape recorder in our house. House belongs to us, so also the tape recorder. Then the volume should be moderate and should not play like public addressing system. No. We don't pay attention to this. Since we like to play it loud, we play it. We don't care to know that this does not fit for minimum civilised behaviour.

It happens even when a person dies.Why to play music while taking the dead body in procession to cremation ground? Why fire works? Is it a celebration? Or is it anything approved by shastras? Nothing. It is sheer madness.

Stricken with grief, silence should predominate. It is terrible to have shattering sounds on this occasion. Startling the public and frightening the people on the street is to be condemned. We should think once why we are showing off thus? It is a mad act that does not give a thought to what the neighbours and people of the town say of the dead man.

If we really loved that dead person, we should take up tasks that will give peace to his soul. One should not plan useless showiness that causes inconvenience to all. There should be sympathy for the relatives of the dead person. Death should not be treated like marriage.

PRESENT IS THE BEST

We should do all the good deeds when our mental and physical health is in order. If time is spent in a lot of hesitation and calculation, that will be too late. There is no point in regretting it later.

We colour our grey hair and assure ourselves. If eyes are dimmed, we conquer it with spectacles. If legs are not cooperating, we take the help of a staff and assure ourselves we are not old yet. We don't recognise that all these characteristics indicate on coming old age.

Tomorrow is unnecessary. The most important thing is to do what we can do today itself.

Another strange thing is we know everything. When it comes to practising, it poses a big problem. We get into a dilemma what to do and what not to do. We are good people. We get good thoughts. Let us implement them as soon as we get them. Instead of endless thoughts a little thing implemented will do us a lot of good.

Those who spend their time in empty words are not workers themselves. Those who cannot do anything but abuse those who are doing are utterly useless. Why should we belong to a category like this?

It is better to be ordinary people with hard work than to be intellectuals who weave a magic with their words. This way we can indeed achieve wonders.

ONLY GOOD NEWS IS GIVEN PERSONALLY

Human welfare is the goal of ever developing science. It is the ultimate aim of science to let people know in minutes whatever is happening in the universe.

Mass media have the responsibility of bringing awareness among people by explaining things and warning them beforehand about the action to be taken when needed.

On the contrary the media are exaggerating things and showing death whether it is natural or accidental on the front page in colour pictures. Certainly it is not their intention to say philosophically that man is mortal after all.

If the country is in chaos the newspapers sell well and make money. If everything is going smooth and fine where is the need for news? So if something undesirable happens mass media seem to be pleased.

In our country high standard newspapers do not smudge their front pages with colour. They do not wait for deaths and road accidents. Giving wide publicity to diseases which have no medicines is meaningless.

In fact we do not want to listen to good words. We are all ears for bad words and rumours. Yes it is our weakness that is becoming their strength.

Wise men said that the news of death should spread silently and not loudly in an entertaining way. Only those who are concerned should know, not the whole world. Why are the provincial newspapers being published?

Bad should not cross limits. Good should not have boundaries.

DESTINATION IS PREDETERMINED

Sometimes we act very foolishly. We are anxious before we set out on a journey to a new town. We are equally anxious to get back to our own place. We are in a great hurry to board the bus or to get off a train.

Though we know we have to get off at the last station we jostle with one another. We want to get down first even if it causes inconvenience to others. We behave the same way in the aeroplane as well.

We get up as soon as the plane comes to a standstill on the runway. We know it takes some time for the ladder to arrive. Yet we don't wait. Though there is no way to get down we stand up impatiently as if some one is punishing us. What for this meaningless haste? We neither gain nor lose time in this process.

There is yet another strange behaviour among us. When we travel by train during night we take many precautions. We clean our berth, spread our bed, adjust fans, keep water bottle near by, change into night dress and make sure our belongings are secure.

Without sparing a thought for others we spread our things and behave as if we own that berth and make fuss as though we are spending a life time there. If we reflect we know all these are foolish deeds.

There may be many differences between man and man in wealth, position and status. There are no economic constraints for good behaviour, good attitude and tolerance. All are eligible to become good human beings. So let us leave aside mean acts and try to become good people.

BEAR DARKNESS TO GIVE LIGHT

We want to be at peace. We want to have a tranquil life. We should be free from anger and other emotions. But all these are our desires.

Since we don't want to stagnate we continue to work in the chosen field. We also get hurt in the process. Yet we go on because we want to reach the goal.

Whatever we may do, whatever we may not do, the one that grows with certainty is age. Whether we want it or not we certainly reach the door step of death. Since we know the fact we continue to work to achieve what we want. In this struggle we lose peace and calm.

No way to perfection is smooth and easy. We are disturbed. We are upset that there is not enough time. Under these circumstances anger and annoyance accompany us. We get upset when things do not happen the way we want them to happen. Yet we do not relent. In this process there is a chance of hurting others.

Some become enemies. It is not humanly possible to be concerned about everything and to please everyone. Even if we don't do anything, even if we don't hurt anyone we have to face criticism. They count us among useless people.

A person who is useful to several others cannot be useful to himself. A person who spreads peace has to do it at the cost of his own peace. Yet he is the hero who can uplift the society.

A person who cares for his own happiness is an ordinary man. A person who works for others is an extraordinary man.

THE WEIGHTS HAVE CHANGED

Before marriage we are all great actors. We care for our health. We see that we don't gain weight and remain slim. We are smartly dressed and show our respect for elders.

"Grandma, how are you?", "Uncle, do you have good crop this time?", "Brother, how is your business doing?" are our friendly queries to people around. We try to win their goodwill by showing our concern for their well-being.

We try to impress others by pretending to be busy. We make them believe that we are not interested in other things except our studies. We hide the fact that we smoke and go to movies.

Not knowing all facts about us a girl's father is deceived. Since all our relatives and friends give a good account of us he gives his daughter in marriage.

There was a time when only family background and a person's character counted. So it became important to project oneself as a person with good character. But now only status and earnings acquired importance. No one is bothered about good or bad.

American alliances are wonderful things. Doctors and computer engineers have great demand. Employed people get first preference. We are not bothered about boy's character. We actually marry our daughter to his income.

By choosing this wrong path we make our child suffer, we shed copious tears and are bed ridden with grief. Thus we put an end to ourselves.

A person with good character is as powerful as a leaf of sacred basil in legendary weighing of Sri Krishna.

DON'T INTERFERE

We want everything.We are curious about everything. We want to know even if it means bothering others. This way we only become cheap and nothing is achieved.

First when we get curious, we should decide whether it is necessary or not. To think we should know everything, what is wrong in knowing, is a wrong attitude.

When two people are conversing, we interfere giving our opinion, "Why so? Why don't you do this way?" In the beginning they may be tolerant and answer our queries. But we continue to bombard them with questions.

They get irritated. If we don't recognise this and continue in our own way, they abuse us."Why do you bother? How are you interested in our affairs?" Then we feel humiliated.

Why should we get into a situation like this? We are respected when we are in our limits. Interfering unnecessarily with affairs of others will cheapen us. People avoid us. We should see that people are happy with our presence instead of cursing, "What a plague!"

We should know what we want to know by our own effort. We should not depend on others for everything. If we are too curious, we are humiliated. If we have self control, we come to know everything on its own.

WE SHOULD NOT BE ALL IN ALL

We fear everything. We are worried about yesterday. We are confused about today and anxious about tomorrow. We are losing peace in every matter. We are entertaining meaningless thoughts and confusing ourselves. Especially regarding money, if we have it there is fear, if we don't have it again there is fear. This way everyone with money or without money is restless.

Apart from human beings there are crores of other creatures which are dwelling the earth. Human mind is far superior to all. But all other creatures are living peacefully. Only we are worried about "tomorrow". Instead of living a happy life with our mind, we are becoming restless and insecure.

It is unnecessary to be anxious about earning for children and grand children.

They are robbing us of peace and comfort.

Our children should work hard. They should lead their own life. They should earn their money. They should see ups and downs in life. But it is not correct for us to undergo hardship on their behalf and to earn money for them. This way, we are making our children lazy and robbing them of their life's pleasures.

We should give them a hand till they learn to walk. Afterwards they can stand on their own. Each one who comes into this world has to have his share of labour. Because of hardwork only we will know what comfort is. If they don't know hardships, they don't know comfort also. We can know the comfort also. We can know the comfort of the shade only when there is hot sun.

IF WE LOSE WE HAVE TO CHASE

We have developed a tendency to take everything lightly. We stopped responding to good or bad. When we happen to know of a disaster we tend to say, "Oh it is common nowadays." We don't oppose injustice. We are indifferent to others affairs.

Leave alone big things, we are not responding even to smaller things.

If anyone writes a letter just enquiring about our well-being we don't send a reply. We think "What is there to reply." It is true there is not much letter writing nowadays. But we are also neglecting those who are genuinely concerned about us. This way human relations are affected.

We have impudence to think that everyone writes a letter or makes a phone call with a selfish motive and we on our part has nothing to do with them. Because of this we are ruining the good relations with others.

We have arrogance to think that only others are benefited by us and we have nothing to gain from them. All days are not our days. However big or small a person may be inter depence is inevitable.

In status and economic standards one may be high or low but everyone is helpful to us. It is essential to keep in mind that if we look down on anybody we are the ultimate losers.

YOUR LIFE IS YOUR OWN

We are tempted to be like others instead of being ourselves. We choose a work which others have chosen and we think that is the right way. We go with the crowd. We do not understand that this will hide the truth.

Hardly we ask,"Why? And what?" "Since others are doing, we will also do and that is the right thing," is our attitude and we imitate others. We don't have our own individuality.

We never question why this way, why not the other way. So we are blindly following instead of searching for the new.

We underestimate ourselves. We can't think that we too can think creatively and can start ideal jobs. We are giving up broadmindedness. We are afraid to follow a new path thinking it as a risk. We are not inaugurating any new turn. We can't even think we have an individuality of our own. How unfortunate! How painful it is not to have courage to achieve anything.

What is so great about doing the same that the other person does? What is our talent? We need our own thoughts. We should implement them with discernment. Then only we can progress and be models to others.

DEDICATION IS NEEDED

Recently I met a person. He had very clear ideas about education of his children. He has two boys. He says he will not send them even for primary education. I asked him why?

He said, "We are three boys to our parents. We lost our father in our childhood itself. My mother faced many hardships to educate us. Two of us studied upto tenth. The third one completed his degree. We didn't have any employment. So we started working as daily wage earners.

Even this we are not able to do well because of our education. If we were working in the fields since childhood we would have become experts and been better off. Unnecessarily, we troubled our mother for fifteen years because of our education"

He further continued, "There are no jobs even for higher education. A little education would leave us no where either as wage earners or as employees. That's why I will not educate my children."

First I thought it was a horrible decision. On contemplation, I found he was correct in his own way.

Just as half knowledge confuses a man, a little education incapacitates him from doing justice either to physical labour or to a white-collared job. I don't mean to say education is a waste. But our education should not be a hindrance for earning our livelihood. The person who respects his profession in spite of having no relationship between his education and job gets respected in turn.

LEAVE SOME SPACE

We think everything is essential.Each and everything, every paper looks important. So we keep them all safe. The whole house, table drawers, shirt and pants, pockets all get filled with papers. We think they are very important. So tuck them somewhere.

Later on, we can weed out.But we don't do that. Whichever paper we may pickup, we think that is very important. Pickup anything for discarding. After thought comes, "It will be useful sometime." So things are accumulated. "Who knows when a thing is useful?" So we madly collect things.

Because of this, we cannot get hold of anything when we want. We search the whole house. "Whatever happened to that? We kept it here only, "we say and start pulling our hair. But it is of no use. It is not only things and papers. If we fill our brain also with useless things and convert it into a wastepaper basket, then all important things will go to oblivion. As a result, we will be devoid of any intelligence.

We should have a review now and then. Whether it is a thing or a subject, discernment is necessary. When we feel that it is important, we keep it safe. That is all right. When we think something is not necessary, we should throw it away.

It is absolutely essential to paint the house and to cleanse the mind.

WE CAN'T HIDE IT

Always we strive to please others, to win their love, to have the partonage of influential people and develop friendship with them. For that, we generally say things which please them. We try to flatter them.

We know all these are untruths. We think we have trapped the people with our words. This may work for a while but does not work for long. This experiment will boomerang. Then we will be depicted as liars.

Infact, we want to tell them the truth. We hesitate thinking that the others may be offended. But this is not the real situation. Even they want our sincere opinion. Perhaps they may be embarrassed initially. But that is no reason why we should resort to lies. It is also impossible to be Satya Harischandra to abide by truth. But how insufferable it is to tell lies for every small thing!

The other person will underestimate us. He can't withstand our presence. He wants to get rid of us. Do we like to be looked down like that? Why should we be in this plight?

Infact, there is no one who has come up in life because of lies. That is why they say truth triumphs.

CONSCIENCE PRICKS THE HEART

We have love. We are also love crazy. Excessive love for others is troublesome to us as well as others. Everything should have limits. It is said that one should give up extremity in anything. Yet our heart leaps with excessive love.

When children don't return home on time we get anxious. Suppose we express our anxiety when they are back they are irritated. "Why were you afraid? Am I still a child?" We get hurt. He does not recognise our love. The hurt is not for he not recognising love. It is for not understanding our fear which is natural for a loving heart.

Even when the wife asks, "Why so many cigarettes? Where had you been till this late hour?" We are irritated though it is about our health she is worried about we retort. "Enough, what are these enquiries and interrogation?" We don't understand that it is natural for her to be anxious about our health. We behave rudely.

Neighbours, relatives and friends too have love for us depending on proximity. Sometimes we don't particularly care. So we are indifferent to those who love us and those whom we love are indifferent to us.

All people cannot approach the waves of the sea.Some are afraid. It does not mean they do not care for the sea. All cannot appreciate excessive love. Some how they are frightened. They agree that the other person is good but try to evade him. Love is a costly affair.

WINNERS DO THINGS DIFFERENTLY

Some people do not have enough time. Some others do not know what to do with their time. We have people who do not work but not the people without work. Of course a slothful person has nothing to do at all.

A useless person harms himself as well as those around him.

A useful person is alone but strives for many people giving light and driving away darkness.

Concentration is essential for an achiever. He always contemplates on his duty. An envious person tries to disturb him. He uses many cunning ways to distract the achiever.

For such people their tongue itself is their weapon. His finger is always pointed towards us obstructing our work. We have such people plenty around us. They hang upside down like bats spying on our movements as if it is their regular duty.

They don't know what work to do. They waste their time by frivolous talk and most part of the day is spent in criticising others. A day will come when they will be a burden to themselves and will be treated as good as dead.

So let us not be like them by keeping our head firmly on our shoulders. Our head has its own value. Our view has its own value. Our work has its own value.

Our mind has its own value. We should uphold our values and never discard them as clothes. Winners don't do different things. They do things differently.

A LOVING HEART

Once my friend, his daughter and I were having our dinner. My friend's friend was also there with us. My friend is extremely fond of his daughter.

While the daughter was having her food, the father's eyes were very observant noticing what she was eating. At one point she was about to reach for pickle. Her father said, "Leave it. Try this dish. It is very tasty." The girl left the pickle and tried the dish suggested by her father.

My friend's friend was furious. He said, "You say you love your daughter a lot. Is it the way you love her? You won't let her eat freely. Let her eat what she wants. I have not seen a father as dictatorial as you are."

My friend was taken aback and was speechless. Seeing all this I wondered what is this all about. Only when we love a person we get anxious and take extra care.

Even when the other person says enough we insist he should have a little more. So here also it was love and not any bad intention of forcing or ordering the other person.

Even when children grow up they always remain children for their parents. The argument that they have their own individuality does not count here.

Those who cannot understand this subtlety distort every word and every deed and spoil the atmosphere.

It is better to have an agonised heart of love than to have a stable balanced approach. Devotion and submission are two flowers that need to be placed before personification of love.

YOU ARE ANSWERABLE TO YOURSELF

We unnecessarily think of the world a lot. When we want to do a thing, we hesitate thinking what people will say. On many occasions, we are afraid. Sometimes we do things which are not to our liking, for the sake of society. Fearing public opinion, we sometimes give up things contrary to our conscience.

Indeed who cares for us? Each one is busy with his own problems. If we do something new, then news spreads. At best they may talk about it for a week. Then everyone will get busy with their own work. By then, news will be old. For this much we are living all our life for others.

If we commit any mistake, we have to fear society. We should fear the world if we do wrong.When we continue to do good according to our method, then we need not care for anyone.

We may talk in front of anybody. To go ahead without fear or favour should be our aim.We are just agitated saying, "Society, society" but have they ever come to single opinion? No. One person does not agree with another person.

Can we satisfy everyone in everything? I don't mean to say one doesn't need to listen to anybody and be obstinate. There is a general practice in society which we normally follow. So it is futile to be worried about society for everything. Our conscience is our witness. Our act will give us adequate result.

YOU NEED YOURSELF

The world does not want a happy man. It wants a successful man. Many people think that life is meant only for money and not for happiness and comfort. When victory turns into a defeat, no one understands him. No sympathy is shown and he is looked down.

Having realised this secret, we should try to be a happy man. Successful man will come later. Moreover, it is a socially related term.

Happy man is our personal matter.It is not important how grandly we lived, in how many cars we moved and how many bungalows we owned.

It is important if we lived without hurting and exploiting others and causing incovenience to them. We don't have any right to hurt anybody in this world. Similarly we have a right to live happily.

Infact, what we need are comfort and happiness. The peace we get out of this can be disseminated among others. If our own life is chaotic, what can we do for our family or society? It is a beautiful lie to think that we are working for others and living for others. It is hypocrisy to talk tall.

Happiness and comfort can never be reduced by distributing among others. So let us be happy and the success will come along.

BE TRUE TO THY OWN SELF

We have several needs. We cannot fulfil all of them on our own. So we have to depend on others.We have to seek many people's help. There is nothing wrong in it.

Some people do not help even though they are in a position to help. But they give false hope saying, "Let us see, let us do." It is a waste to trust these people and to entertain any hope.

When those who are naturally helpful and capable promise, "I will certainly do it" we should not doubt their intention. But in our anxiety we do not want to take any chance. So we approach yet another person.

Similarly we approach a few more people. Till our work is done we continue to pester them without allowing as much as breathing time.

Someone is kind enough to get our work done. Our need is fulfilled. From then onwards our nature itself changes.

We do not thank any person saying, "Because of you my work is done." Even if we say so outwardly, we don't have any feeling of gratitude in our heart.

We arrogate ourselves thinking, "Time was in my favour. So my work is done. How did these people help me?" This meanness has only one reason– we do not trust anyone. It is a result of approaching and crawling before everyone to get our work done.

A person who moves with several people for selfish reasons, a person who cannot be faithful to anyone can have no one to call his own. Ultimately he cannot trust even his own self.

SHOULDN'T WE CRY IN PAIN?

We have become very indifferent. Our reaction to good or bad is considerably reduced. Suppose someone criticises us we may not care.

We are not happy either when others praise us. It does not mean we have attained equanimity towards happiness and unhappiness.

We are not simply interested in many things that are happening around us. We have adopted the attitude, "How does it matter to me?" A human heart should have a certain reaction. One must be able to cry or laugh whole heartedly.

We can't love people with our frozen hearts. Nor do we get their love in return. If we are sensitive we can follow good path. Only a sensitive heart has creative power.

We think cheating and falsehood are prevalent every where. We firmly believe that there are no good people. This kind of attitude does not help us grow.

It becomes an obstacle to our progress. Shedding tears when bad happens and smiling when good happens is natural to human beings.

If someone felicitates us recognising our talent we should feel happy. To express gratitude we have to say a few words in the meeting. If words fail atleast one should be able to shed tears of joy. If a person remains unmoved like a statue he should be counted as a hard hearted person.

We know how to run away when stones are pelted. We have yet to know how to be thrilled by a shower of flowers.

THERE IS BEGINNING IN THE END

We bring up children and when they grow up, we marry them off. Each one goes one's own way. They earn their livelihood. At last the couple remains and think, "We have become lonely."

Though they live together under one roof, husband and wife lead lonely lives. "What is left there? Life is over. Why does the world need us?" is the strange philosophy adopted.

Spiritless life goes on. Because we think marriage is for getting children and the life's responsibility is over once the children are married and settled in life, we feel we are in a vacuum.

Why should it happen this way? Why should we think that life is over and nothing more is to be done? Life starts with husband and wife. Children grow up and leave. Now again husband and wife remain. That means the same as the newly weds. Then why don't we have the same enthusiasm as we had in the beginning? We should start life afresh like the newly weds. We should take up new works with matured minds and plan many good deeds. With the experience and acquired wisdom, many useful things should be started and we should live a carefree life.

Life does not mean only difficulties and responsibilities. There is much more interesting part. That we should experience. Only the one who is leading a comfortable life, can shoulder the responsibilities more effectively and efficiently.

LET US SPEAK MOTHER TONGUE ALSO

Elders say that we should speak of our country wherever we go. We hesitate even to mention our mother tongue, let alone patriotism.We are not speaking Telugu in Telugu land anyway. Even in a foreign land when two Telugu people meet, they don't speak Telugu even to remind themselves that both of them are Telugu people.

We don't become great just because we can speak other languages.We don't be lowly because we speak in mother tongue.Greatness doesn't belong to the language.It belongs to the meaning that emerges out of mind.

Just as a companion brings a lot of happiness when we cry in wilderness, we should experience similar happiness when we meet our language speaking people in an alien land. But we mask our happiness with useless poses. We have come to a state that even the trouble of the heart is to be conveyed in an alien language. We may learn any number of languages but when we experience pain, we utter a cry in our own language. Our mother tongue is there in our blood, life and every atom of our body. That is why we should be able to talk in mother tongue with pride.

When I visited different countries and met important people, I mostly observed only Telugu people not speaking their mother tongue. The fault lies with us. This trend is mainly responsible for our language not getting its due recognition. Elevation of children should please mother. It should be realised that speaking Telugu means respecting our Telugu land. It is not in children's nature to humiliate their mother.

IT IS GOOD TO RELENT

We are obstinate. We also have self-importance. We can achieve things only when we are relentless and capable. So far so good. But at times we are very stubborn. We don't tolerate any one accusing us. We are very angry with them.

This results in increasing the distance between the two. As time passes there is more anger and harshness. We may at times think, "I have done no wrong. Let me take initiative to be good," but our ego comes in between. We also suspect that others may look down on us. With that we become stiff.

A humble person alone gets respect.The one who moves about arrogantly will be ultimately humiliated and will be lonely in his agony.

What do we achieve in life if we distance ourselves from our own people and people who love us? Both parties are right and wrong in someway or the other.

There is no point in thinking, "I am perfect" which is not the attitude of wise people.

A waterfall comes down from the mountains above. It does not mean it has fallen from heights. Similarly in order to maintain good relations with people coming down from our heights only shows our maturity.

A person who relents alone can hold his head high. When we walk on the grass it bends and the moment we lift our foot it stands upright.

Bending is its humility. Standing upright is its character. That is what we also need.

YOUR GOAL IS YOUR OWN

We try to impose our likes and dislikes on others. We impose them on those who are humble and dependent on us. We direct them to practise all these things.

There can be many reasons why we don't like many things. Some may not be suitable to us. These are all our personal matters. It is a mistake to think what we do is good and what we don't do is bad.

We can't say "no" to any liking or disliking. No one knows why and what of it. It depends on one's physical and mental traits.

For example we get up early in the morning and go for a walk. That is necessary for us. But because morning walk is good for health we should not wake up every member in the family and force them to go for walk. This is nothing but exhibiting our ego as the head of the family.

We are growing old and it is all right for us to go for morning walk. Why should we wake up the children from deep sleep and force them to go for walk?

Did we go for regular walks when we were of their age? Didn't we enjoy long hours of sleep? This kind of tyrannical trends are not appreciated either at home or outside. There is no meaning in forcing old age habits on the young. Each age has its own pleasure.

We are respected when we are within our limits. When we cross the limits the other person can oppose us. One should be cautious not to get into that kind of situation.

WE ARE AMIDST GOOD PEOPLE

Whenever we are in trouble we tell ourselves, "These days no work can be done without lying. It is not possible to earn money without cheating. Existence is difficult if we are not corrupt. The whole world is like that.

"All are doing the same. We should go along with others. Otherwise we cannot survive. The time is not favourable to the righteous." But these opinions are not correct.

If we observe the world we know what is true and what is not true. A bad man cannot be a great man. He has no place and happiness.

When we observe keenly we see many good people around us. They live with peace and happiness. Even though they don't live in large palatial houses they don't live in want. Their children and whole household are healthy.

Their good conduct, their righteous attitude continue to protect them. People around us, a large number of them, live trusting truth, justice and righteousness. If we set aside some weaknesses and a few temptations majority of the population trusts goodness.

Whenever we are faced with hardship, when our expectations are belied we tend to say, "The world is ruined." But it is not true. Are we living only among bad people? No. Only a small percentage may be termed as bad.

They have their own troubles. But we wonder whether they have any hardships at all. We don't understand that only they have all kinds of troubles. The justice and righteousness that protect us are within us only and they continue to be with us.

WE ARE PUNISHING OURSELVES

There is some meaning in suffering with illness and fearing a disease. But it is painful to imagine various diseases and to be perpetually in fear.

It is good to wish that our body should be healthy and to take necessary precautions towards that.

On the contrary, when there is no disease, when doctors conduct tests and assure, "You are perfectly all right. Nothing to worry," still getting worked up and to think one is ill, is our own misfortune. This is a new disease we ourselves are inviting.Since there is no medicine for this mental illness, our life will become hell.We are confused not knowing what to eat, what not to eat, what to do and what not to do.

It is not good to have either tea or coffee. Lady's finger causes wind, bitter gourd causes bile, tamarind causes cold and every other vegetable has some evil. Then what do we eat and how do we survive? Even the environment is polluted.

So if they warn us not to breathe in cities, can we live without breathing?

Each thing has both good and bad. To see what suits our body is more important than seeing what the science says.

We should do a job which is suitable to our mental make-up. Similarly the best thing is to eat what suits our body and leave what is unsuitable.

NO THRIFT IN LOVE

Elders say that we should have a feeling of fraternity towards everyone. It is good to have this feeling instead of having enmity.But these days, brothers themselves are fighting. There are many differences between blood-brothers. Envy and hatred are growing. The records say that nowadays most of the cases in the courts are between brothers.

People get befriended and at the height of their friendship, they introduce each other as, "My brother." Now meanings and values are changing for words like brother and sister.

In the past, when one is told to treat the fellow being as brother or sister, it only meant to have unity and love as used to be between brothers and brother and sister. But the fact is quite contrary. How nice it would be if the same warm relations continue between people as they were sometime ago!What more happiness do we need than to live in unity?

There is a feeling which is better than that of a feeling of fraternity. That is to extend to others the same love, care and devotion we have for ourselves. This is a wonderful thing to happen.

If we start feeling the same pain for others as we feel for ourselves when we are hurt, then this loving feeling will convert man into God. We should look after others as we look after ourselves.

WASTE NOT, WANT NOT

As soon as we are settled economically, we think of owning a house. We think we shall be happy with a house that meets our needs.

If we leave a few exceptions, usually many of us save and borrow money to own a house. Though we know the troubles of borrowing money we overcome them with an expectation of owning a house.

This is the time when we becomes victims of *Vaastu*. All types of experts on *Vaastu* start visiting us.

Each one has his own interpretation. We are confused not knowing what to do and what not to do.

When a disease is diagnosed the medical science prescribes only one cure. A science is accurate wherever it is written. But these *Vaastu* experts don't tell us what criteria they are following. They threaten us saying if wedon't follow their instructions we shall be courting trouble.

Since we cannot tackle them all we trust one person. Now he will take us for a ride. So we should see how reasonable and true his suggestions are and accept them with discretion. If we follow him blindly that will spell our ruin.

We do not know whether we get wealth if we follow *Vaastu* but surely we will encounter financial crisis. So it is essential to follow *Vaastu* principles as far as our limited resources and scope permit so that we may live in comfort.

YOU ALONE ARE THE DOER

We always underestimate ourselves. We don't have self confidence to think we can do great things and we can achieve even impossible things. Since we have this feeling of inferiority we think the other person is a great person.

Even if the other person is great we don't lose anything. But looking down upon ourselves will not allow us to grow. So we foolishly think we are all right as we are.

We don't understand how harmful this feeling is. This nature will make us a coward at every point.

That makes us depend on others. We seek solace from them. We crave to be approved by others. Why are we undergoing this trouble? We have enough strength to fight. We have capabilities to achieve success.

Though equipped with everything we live as though we are deprived of everything. We should have introspection. We should examine ourselves. We should accept our own short comings and bad traits. If we don't have any there is no need to be ashamed of ourselves.

We don't lack good qualities, honesty and ethics. We have enormous capabilities and intelligence. So we are like an impregnable fort and we are capable persons.

When we get rid of cowardice courage becomes our own. The tail cannot wag a dog. A dog can wag the tail. Without knowing this we get confused that perhaps the tail may wag the dog.

We are the only people who can, who will and who should be doing whatever we want to do.

X-RAY OF A HANDSOME PERSON IS ALSO UGLY

It is all right if one thinks he is very intelligent. But it is our ignorance to think the other person is not intelligent. Perhaps we acquire by birth this talent of underestimating others and finding fault with their words and deeds. We are ready to criticize each and everyone.

"Oh, I could have done better than that. God knows what he does, no one can make out head or tail of it. He does not know subtlety. He can't understand easy method."

We are eloquent, give free advice and are happy with ourselves. "See the way I talk. The other guy is awe struck and is listening to everything I say. A fool indeed."

So we revel in our greatness. We don't understand that the other person is being tolerant towards us. If someone challenges us saying, "Why all this talk. You take up any of my tasks and prove your ability", we have no answer.

We mistake people's goodness as their incapability. We are such insignificant ants who don't have this much knowledge that one's capability is shown not in words but in deeds. It is very difficult to understand intellectuals and get into the depths of their thought to get the correct meaning. But our acts of superiority complex are quite revealing.

People can easily understand that this attitude is crooked and narrow. The one who boasts of his capabilities is an inferior person. The person who can achieve and show it to others is a great person.

NO ONE WALKS THE MOMENT ONE IS BORN

We are capable of talking rudely. We can also take horrible decisions. Because we never remember our past. We take into account what happened at present.

We have to live in present. We should continue with our duties. But today's work can be done based on the past experience. For example a surgeon performs operations every day. He removes pain and saves many lives.

But we have to take note of something here. His past helped him to become an experienced surgeon. Many teachers had taught him. His parents too did their duty and helped him. This should not be forgotten.

Let us suppose someone abused us or hit us. Immediately we complain it to someone else. The other person will say it is unjust. Then he will think the person who attacked us is a bad person.

If we take into account only beating part, that is indeed brutal. But we tend to forget to ask a few questions.

It is essential to ask "Why did he beat you? Did you provoke him by your act, word or deed?"

No one commits wrong just like that. Another person is also responsible for conflict and fight. While yesterday gave birth to today, today undergoes labour pains to give birth to tomorrow.

A LITTLE LAMP DRIVES AWAY DARKNESS

We all crave for comfort and happiness. We hope for longevity, good health and wealth. Our daily struggle is meant only for this.

We think acquiring wealth is very important. We take care of our health thinking that without health everything else is futile. Though we hesitate what food would cause what harm, we tend to neglect ourselves.

We want to be careful in everything yet we are irregular in our daily routine. Sometimes we fall ill because of this, but correct ourselves and move ahead. This way it is common to commit mistakes and to correct ourselves.

We don't give same importance to mental happiness as we give to money and physical health. We think if we are healthy and wealthy happiness will come on its own. In fact mental peace should flow from the mind. Then only we can have tranquillity. Healthy thoughts lead to mental peace and thoughts emerge only from our mind.

Though we know inner happiness cannot be gained from outside factors we run after external things. It is unwise to think we are clean by having a bath while keeping our mind unclean. The evil in a man can be wiped out only by goodness in the heart.

Inner happiness has everything. Health, wealth and all the riches of the world are within us.

A person may be very strong but he may still suffer from unrest. But a person with inner happiness has honesty in his conduct and courage in his daily work.

NO ONE CAN BE JUST LIKE US

Generally we want to have an upper hand over others. We direct everyone to follow our path. Otherwise we find fault with them.

Suppose we like a film and it is not popular with the audience we criticise saying they do not have a good taste. Similarly if a film which we personally do not like becomes very popular with people we call them crazy.

When there is a book exhibition we come across a number of books written on various themes. We like only certain types of books.

We should buy such books and come home. Instead of that staging a black flag demonstration to protest the exhibition of books we don't like is not a wise thing to do.

In fact in our own house all the members do not hold same opinion. If we like something, the wife likes something else. The daughter has one way and the son has a different way. Thus in our own family there is no unanimity. It does not mean we do not have cordiality.

Each one thinks differently and moves differently. Each one has one's own life and one's own personality. It is to be appreciated that everyone tries to preserve one's own personality. When we understand the tastes of others and respect them we are also respected.

Interfering in others affairs, showing dictatorial tendency is not good. Each one is responsible for one's own life. Everyone can look after their own interests.

BALANCE IS IMPORTANT

We always tend to be extreme. Either too much or too little. We don't have much knowledge about goal-oriented effort.

We are naturally careful about money. We don't spend it wastefully. We also practise thrift. Sometimes we even hesitate to switch on a light thinking that it consumes electricity.

It is a mere precaution not to waste money which we need for tomorrow. Nothing wrong in that. We may say anything but nothing has so much importance in this world as money. But that does not mean we have to lead a life of a miser.

It is said that while earning money we should earn as if we were living for ever in this world. But while giving away in charity we should think there is no tomorrow.

In the name of thrift if we become stingy we may feel even our children's food is a waste. "Why that curry? Today this chutney would do" will be the attitude. Then we don't feed them to their satisfaction.

What do we gain by hurting the same children for whose sake we are doing all this? We are creating such circumstances as children themselves will call our attitude miserly and look down on us.

Thrift is good. But it should have some purpose and method. Let not the poor man live like a rich man and a rich man live like a poor man.

MIND IS IMPORTANT

Our ancestors fixed a few traditions with great foresight. They gave importance to health and hygiene and introduced a few conventions.

Since we don't do things just because we are told to do so, they said doing certain things would be beneficial whereas doing certain things would be harmful.

In certain cases they even induced fear in us. Why? They hoped atleast then we would practise right things.

They said the month of Ashada (June-July) is not auspicious for marriages. But we think it is harmful even to discuss marriage during that period. "Our daughter's marriage is almost settled. We will discuss everything in Shravana (July-August)", we say.

Since marriage is good news the other person may ask enthusiastically, "Who is the boy? What does he do? How much is the dowry?"

We reply nonchalantly, "It is not good to discuss these things during Ashada. So we did not talk any details." Does it make any sense?

At the same time we have no objection to avail ourselves of discounts offered by shop keepers during this period. We buy clothes and other items needed for marriage because it is beneficial to us.

We are converting scientific traditions into blind faith. When living itself is becoming hard day by day we are inviting further trouble by creating obstacles for ourselves in the name of tradition.

If we have scientific approach and proper understanding why should we be victims of such groundless fears?

HUMAN BEING IS A SUM TOTAL OF EMOTIONS

It is natural for a human being to have some health problem or the other. It is rare to have a person with perfect health. Even when a person gets a certificate in medical check-up that nothing is wrong with his health, he cannot be sure that nothing would ail him.

Similar is the case with problems. But they can be solved in case they are real problems.

We live in this society along with wife, children,parents, brothers, friends and others. So how can one be free from problems? But we don't see the problems as they are. The real problem is our tendency to look at a small problem as a big one and a big problem as a small one.

When we see problems separately and life separately the problems look magnified. If we approach them that problems are natural and they are part of life, there is no need for anxiety and no place for fear.

A person who sails on the sea too has a problem. But he can travel safely with the help of a compass. The darkness will vanish the moment we light a lamp.

Certain wounds are healed by time alone. Either it is grief or severity of a problem the intensity we have today may not be there tomorrow. Human life is made of complications, irritations, happiness and unhappiness. If these are absent in a person's life he is as good as dead.

Would not a person know how to walk when he knows how to run? Can't a man who has to live hundred years sort out his problems which take only a few days?

THERE ARE MANY THINGS TO BE DONE

We are under the illusion that we are great adventurers and take many risks. We don't board a bus, when it stops at the stand; we would rather board it when it is moving. We try to get down when the bus is on the move. We run to cross the road when the traffic is heavy. Similarly when we drive mopeds, scooters or cars, we drive in great speed and overtake every other vehicle. All these, according to us, are great adventures. If anyone looks in our direction while we are indulging in these acts, we pat ourselves thinking, "What great heroes we are!" In fact ,what we don't realise is that the other person is considering us as very stupid.

We don't help an old woman to cross the road. When a lost child is crying, we don't help him to reach his parents. We don't even remove the obstacles like thorn, stone or banana peel from the path keeping in mind the welfare of other passers by.These things are not visible to us at all.We think these jobs may be done by old people who have no other work. We see in front of us an ant drowning in water. We don't care to save it.

It is horrible to have capacity to save a creature but not save. Even if it is a little help that leads to good result, we should be in the forefront.

It is more important to live than to undertake fatal misadventures. A coward makes his own life miserable. If a misadventurer becomes an adventurer, he will be useful to himself as well as society.

EVEN THE SEA ROARS

It is dangerous to have people who are silent. No one knows what is there on their mind. We don't know their opinion. Silence is their strong weapon. With that, they do things which they ought not be doing.

There are many who do sweet talking. They are cut throats. None feels the pain but one is dead. They speak from their tongue. We speak strongly because it comes from the depth of our heart.

Our words are like thunder before rain. Just as the rain after thunder brings comfort, peace and prosperity, the after effect of our words will be beneficial to the other person. Even animals express their emotions through sounds. But these silent people do not give any indication. If we think they are men of action, yes, they are, but men of bad action.

Why to quiz saying,"Silence is half agreement"? It is all right to speak out frankly. Man has thoughts. He wants to express them. There is a suitable language. Having been so equipped, why should a person be silent?

In this vast creation there are crores of living creatures. Except for human beings, no other creature has capacity to speak. They confine themselves to signs and signals. Let us make good use of this fortune and opportunity of speech in this birth itself.

ASSUMPTIONS ARE HARMFUL

We know it is wrong to lie. Yet we tell lies atleast a dozen times in a day. We know we should be righteous. Yet we behave unrighteously and tell ourselves "This is right according to me."

We know it is not right to do wrong to others. But we say, "What is wrong in it? Everyone is doing the same" and justify ourselves to follow that unjust path.

We know our wrong as well as right deeds. Our conscience pricks us. Yet we suppress the voice of the conscience.

We ourselves decide that this is the way one should follow in this world and select a short cut. We think this is the way to reach our goal or to achieve what we want. But no one can win by following unjust and unrighteous short cuts.

Similarly one should not resort to unjust ways by saying "Only for this time" One should not even ask, "When everyone else is doing the same, why can't I? If I do not follow the way of the world how do I survive? How do I exist?"

However we may look down on the world and its ways, a large number of people follow only just path.Bad people are less in number. The fact is good does not get publicity.

Bad does not need publicity because it spreads like conflagration. If a wrong deed is hidden that burns us like a live coal. The problem ends the moment we confess our mistake.

YOU SHOULD BE VISIBLE IN YOURSELF

We have freedom of speech. We have a right to criticise anyone. We need not hesitate even if they are national leaders. We have this freedom by law. That is why sometimes we are carried away. Stronger is our abuse better we feel. We try to find fault from every aspect and attack them. That is a kind of happiness.

But are we using the same freedom in every case? No. We do not criticise our boss. It is a different matter if we abuse him in our heart of hearts.

If we say anything against the boss we are sure to lose our job. There we control our tongue. So, whatever happened to our freedom of speech?

Why so far? Can we abuse people at home? Can we hurt them by saying harsh things? No. Because they will drive us out of the house. We also abuse God. In our ignorance we think He can do us no harm. Anyway He is silent and does not react. With this assurance we criticise Him. A storm cannot uproot a blade of grass. That is why it stands upright with pride. We are also of the same type.

A person who makes use of his freedom should be same with every one at every place. A person hides his feelings at some place and overtly expresses at some other place is a coward. A person who is different at different times is not a human being at all.

For a courageous man good quality is essential. Good character should be base for that. A person with good qualities and good character is transparent and makes good use of every right.

OUR PATH LEADS TO GOOD GOAL

We know about ourselves. We know what we are capable or incapable of doing. We have a fair understanding of our strengths and weaknesses. Yet we tend to be unclear. So we don't know what we are.

We can't change physical inadequacies.There is no need. Knowing that everyone's mind chooses only good we try to show off our knowledge. Here our mind enters. That distorts every act and every thought.

That is why we are upset about everything and lose mental peace. Our ego comes in the way to admit we are not intelligent. If we do so, we fear, others may look down on us.

A person who can say with courage "I have a mind of my own. I do accordingly" is a clear person.

Intelligence should be able to distinguish between good and bad. Mind has no complications or complexities. It glides smoothly like mercury.

If we follow our mind we can reach our goal. Every act that is done intentionally may not be yielding results for us as well as for others because intelligence may have no discretion. Every act that is done whole heartedly gives us happiness and benefits others.

Much is not lost if we are not intelligent. But a man with out a heart is not suitable to be among human beings.

A THEIST HAS FOUR LEGS

While walking I looked back. I saw two more foot impressions besides mine. "What is this? These two feet belong to whom?" I wondered. There was a little surprise, a little confusion and a little fear.

Then I heard a disembodied voice. "I am the God you trusted. I am always with you protecting you. The foot impressions besides yours are mine."

I was overwhelmed. "Glory to you Lord," I said kneeling.

My life was happy and comfortable. But anything unexpected can happen in life. This happened in my case as well.

My troubles started. All my human efforts failed. I could not tolerate those hardships anymore.

Then I remembered God again. I turned back to see. I saw impressions of two feet only. What is this? There should have been four impressions.

What happened to foot impressions of God. "Oh God, you were with me as long as I was all right. Now that I am in troubles you escaped," I cried and blamed Him for cheating me.

Again I heard a disembodied voice. "Poor fellow! Seeing you in trouble I am bearing you on my shoulders. So your foot impressions are not there on the ground. What you see are my foot impressions."

I cried uncontrollably. I was repentant that I misunderstood that kindness incarnate. "Pardon me Lord, I couldn't understand your ways," I said prostrating.

(Thanks to an anonymous writer)

YOU SHOULD BE ONE WITH THEM

Our life has become a running race. We face severe competition in every field. In this race we are neglecting our own children which is a great mistake. Children are great observers. They have sharp eyes and sharp brain. They ask questions and search for answers. We should give those answers however hard it may be.

Let us accept the truth without fear. The fact is our children can think better than us. We should observe their observation quality. We always think about children from our point of view. We bring their childhood into the scope of adulthood.

We should see childhood as childhood. Helping children grow up does not mean wounding their childhood and tenderness and turning into rock like hardness. We should preserve their tenderness.

We should enable them to understand the world. We should show them all fields and all colours. They should be given opportunity to observe everything thoroughly. This way they can understand themselves and decide what they want for themselves. Our responsibility is to cooperate with them so that they can come to that conclusion.

We have this dictatorial tendency to think that children are younger than us, so they should listen to what we say and work hard for the targets we fix for them.

In fact we should realise that children too have individuality and a mind of their own. The parents who can understand what the children are feeling and what they are thinking are the true parents.

A HAND OF ASSURANCE

In our life the most important thing can never be affected. No injustice will be done. Certainly that important thing would be achieved. But we are worried thinking that we are facing difficulties and all troubles are surrounding us.

Yet we are also comfortable. We also have our joys.If we think of only troubles what do we gain except grief. If our life is only made of troubles how are we existing? In fact we have more joys than sorrows.

When one is not hungry even the best dish has no taste for him. When one is hungry gruel too looks appetizing. When we cannot sleep even the most comfortable bed cannot induce sleep. When we are sleepy even the hard ground is good enough.

Without realising this we crave for a comfortable bed and exotic dish and feel miserable when we cannot get them.We should understand that whatever happens that is happening for our own good. Whatever we have they are our valuable things.

Just as there is no perfect human being there cannot a life filled only with riches.Every person has something lacking. By contemplating on that one thinks life is full of pain. We leave out many plus points and hold on to one minus point which results in misery.

If we think for a while we understand that we are what we are today because that most important thing in our life is in tact. Our thoughts should flow from the strong foundation of faith. No one is ruined because of trust.

ONLY A FRESH FLOWER IS VALUED

In the countries I have visited hosts are more respected than guests. But in our country guests are respected by a house holder. That is why we say "A guest is God Himself."

The guest accepts our hospitality and blesses us in return. There are some who arrive at meal time unannounced. We consider him as God and extend our hospitality. This is the unique tradition of this country.

Nowadays the meaning of guest has changed. Guest is one who will not be a pest.

But as guests we do not realise this. We stay on and on enjoying their hospitality without realising their difficulties. In between we enquire with great civility. "Are we disturbing you? Hope we are not obstructing your work. Please be frank so that we may leave." But we continue to stay on as long as we please.

Outwardly we show our respect but in fact we tread on their toes.

A guest should be so endearing that the other person should look forward to our next visit. Even though they say, "Please stay for a day more" we should not be tempted.

Because anyway we have to leave. Why should we stay for so long making others long for our departure? It is better to save our honour by leaving at appropriate time. That is best civility.

WE DO NOT DIFFERENTIATE BETWEEN OUR FINGERS

Sometimes we say, "I am not the type to bend before others. What if somebody had money. I don't need his status, position or name and fame. I will not ask for a favour. I never belittled my individuality."

It is good. No one should be a slave to another. Nevertheless one needs another person's help.

A person can be alone looking after his physical well-being, living in peace and tranquillity away from crowds. But we have a family. There is a society which has high, low and ordinary people. Accordingly we conduct ourselves.

Can we have the same approach to a person who lends money or a person who borrows money? Suppose we have a friend who is a doctor we look at him as a friend when we are not ill. When we fall ill we look up to him as doctor, respect him and look forward to getting cured.

In this case we are not pretending anything. At this moment we have to respect him, trust him and should not have a light attitude just because he is our friend.

If we do so the loss is ours. Similarly we cannot have same attitude and respect for everyone in this world. Each one has a place in society. We should accept their respective positions. Then only each one can be equal to another.

FRUIT FOR ME AND PEEL FOR YOU

It has become a habit with us to pass on the work which we ourselves can do to the person next to us. We adopt the same method whether we are at home or outside.

Even when it comes to neatness we take care of only ourselves. We don't show any interest in household work. We think it is either the work of the housewife or of servants.

Even when we are outside we behave the same. Starting from home, in offices, bus-stands, railway stations, municipal roads we throw waste everywhere.

We are responsible for spreading it. Though thousands of people are responsible for this dirt we leave the cleaning job only to a few.

Can one single person clean up the dirt hundred people have spread? But we are in the forefront to criticise roads and public places. But did we not create this mess?

We oppose the tendency to have one earning member and ten dependants. But we think nothing of lakhs of people littering places and only a few being held responsible for the up keep.

If we do not clean ourselves every day or for that matter as the need arises, our body itself will hate us. That is why we rigorously follow self cleansing routine.

Similarly if we neglect the earth which is our base, the mother earth too will hate us.

GOD'S ABODE IS VERY FAR

Nowadays we don't consider Ram, Shiva or Vishnu as our family deities. Because they are great Gods, they dwell somewhere far off, they have a number of devotees and are not accessible to us. This feeling is unconsciously being absorbed by us.

So, we think it is better to approach a smaller God where not many people throng so that we can make Him hear all our desires. But then what is happening.

There is demand for these smaller Gods as well. So we are approaching godmen because we can talk to them face to face and explain all our problems and find solutions.

Here everything seems to be fine. Not much rush. If we pay adequate money we can worship godman's feet. If we spend a little more money he can come to our place, listen to the desires of all the family members and assure them their desires will be fulfilled. Thus he blesses and goes away.

We think these godmen are better because they respond to our requests. We treat them as our family deities and worship their photographs. It is so convenient that whenever we face a problem we can make a telephone call and tell our God about our problem.

We also get a solution on the phone. What more do we want? If we trust these godmen providing so many facilities life will be smooth and auspicious.

That is why it is said ignorance is bliss.

DOES ONE LOSE A NOSE BY SNEEZING?

We may love ourselves. It is not wrong. But to think that we are unique is our weakness.

We love our body. Our words are like pearls. Our deeds are golden. We don't want to tire our body. Our clothes should not be creased.

Our hair should be in tact. But all the jobs should be done according to our plan. All this is a direct example of selfishness unlimited.

Every small thing we do with a great feeling, "Oh, how hard I am working!" Yet these tasks are not meant for others.These efforts are for our own benefit. It is good to sympathise with others in their difficulties. But to feel pity for ourselves is very mean. It does harm to us. We think it is a calamity to start anything new. With this we become victims of fear and weakness. They leave us as cowards who can't handle anything.

Self-pity leads to unhappiness. It weakens the mind which can face ups and downs of life. It is good to have a soft heart but cowardice is not good. If we treat our body delicately, we can't achieve anything. We will be far away from adventures. Victory will never approach us. Life becomes static. Is it what we want? No.

Human life is meant to progress for ever. Things should not be static. There should be change and that too progressive change. For that one has to work hard and go forward with open eyes.

LIKES AND DISLIKES SHOULD BE LIMITED TO HOME

Just as relationships have changed, so also addressing. There was a time when a wife used to call her husband, "Hello please, would you come here," and the husband used to reply with all politeness, "Yes, I am coming." If the name of the departed father-in-law is given to the child, the mother was never mentioning the boy by name."Where is the second one? He has not come yet?" was the reference. If husband's name is given to her grand children, a woman would never address the boy by name.

They used to give a lot of respect to the name by calling, "That person, this person." Now, things have changed. It is common between husband and wife to insult and abuse each other. These addresses are not confined to themselves. When a husband addresses his wife derogatorily in front of strangers, they feel very embarrassed.

Some address their wives by some other pet names sometimes causing embarrassment to outsiders.

Sometimes between friends also, things change. When they become intimate,for every sentence before and after they add, "Fellow". Why these unnecessary addresses, no one can understand.

This is a civilised society. Whether one likes it or not, one has to follow certain civilities.

A LITTLE CAUTION FOR GREAT BENEFIT

We crave for several tastes. Though we know they lead to physical discomfort our craving for taste defeats us. The things that start as fun later become addictions.

These addictions change our character itself. If we give them an inch they will take a mile. Since some tastes and habits are dangerous we should try to stop their entry itself.

But is it easy to conquer our senses? No. They always take the lead. If we rebel against them they also rebel in turn and create a terrible reaction. We should persuade them to be under our control.

One has to request them saying, "O senses! If I fulfil your cravings my physical health gets affected.Consequently I have to suffer a lot in future. Possible I may die thus suffering. Please don't kill me."

No doubt we don't have control over birth or death but we should remain happy and comfortable as long as we live. It is hell to live a life of suffering. We should not ask for a life where we die every day.

It is all right to argue, "One gets diseases even without bad habits", but it does not avert danger.

We cannot achieve what we want if we are unwell. Even though we have great intellect it is essential to have the cooperation of the body.

We can fulfil our ambitions and ideas only when we have control over our tastes and habits.

A SMALL BULB LIGHTS UP THE WHOLE ROOM

"Can one person better the country? How does it help if he does not sully himself? These days when everyone is corrupt, when being unjust is treated as social virtue, what can this single person do?" Thus we express our disappointment. Moreover, we make fun of those who are honest.

But we know how a responsible officer with his honesty sent shivers through the spines of many a leader. So one should not worry that a person is alone.One leader is enough to keep the country on the right track.

It is enough if one person stands up for all.Then everyone will stand by him and cooperate with him. They hail him and protect him like an armour. So if one person is good, he can change the society, country and the world at large. There is no doubt about it. There is nothing to hesitate about being honest.

Didnot one opposed to non-violence win independence for us? Did not one despot bring upon the world war? One person is enough for good or bad.

There may be any number of bogies. Without an engine, they cannot move. There may be any number of people. If there is no able leader, their capabilities will not be known. We know many organizations. If there is change in management, the organization steeped in losses can earn profits and be successful. So each one is a capable person. But a group of people needs leadership. A ship needs a compass and a society needs a selfless person.

DON'T SAY I AM CORRECT, YOU ARE RIGHT

To a large extent there are quarrels, difference of opinion and fights between husband and wife because they come together from two different back grounds.

The atmosphere she grew by, the people and mentalities are different. His customs and thoughts are different.

When both of them start living together, certainly they need some adjustments. It takes some time to understand each other. Somewhere one has to compromise. If such difference of opinion occurs between friends, one gives up that friendship. One can distance oneself from relatives. With neighbours one becomes silent and gets busy with one's own work.

If there is a difference between parents and children, they live separately. When it comes to husband and wife, none of these things is possible because they have to live together throughout life. Because of that anxiety to become one, the quarrels manifest.

Either good or bad, household matters or outside matters or just a **tete-a-tete,** it is the couple which will be talking with each other.Theirs is never ending conversation. However different or indifferent they may be, their bond will bring them together.

Their togetherness does not have any secrets or reservations. To neglect such an important life partner is a punishment which we impose on ourselves.

SOWING GOOD IS OUR DUTY

All minds are clear to start with. By nature no one is born with a bad mind or a good mind. Gradually according to our capacity we pollute it. Even when we know we have gone astray we defend ourselves saying, "This is what my life taught me. This society changed me like this."

Every person is a mixture of good and bad. If we are good to others they will be good to us. When we do bad we get punished for that. There may be delay but everyone will get justice and injustice will end.

It is natural to expect results after hard work. Sometimes we may not get the result we wanted. It does not mean we have to stop working. We should continue with our work.

There is no doubt that we will get the result at appropriate time.

When we are in a position to help others we should help. We should not worry if the other fellow would be grateful or not. He may be grateful. He may be benefited or he may incur losses.

It is good enough to be in a position to help others. One should not think to help is to do charity. Nevertheless when we do good we reap good.

When we are helpful to others, this is an investment which will yield good results in future. We should do good for others for our own good.

CALM THE MIND

In day to day work we bring in an order. From getting up at a particular time till we sleep we follow some method or the other. Whether it is work we do or food we eat we have a particular routine to follow.

That means without our knowledge we fix our life in a frame. If anything happens different we get upset. All this depends on our mental make up. Our own opinions and tastes are also formed like this. Tolerance and intolerance too emerge out of it.

An evening appointment disturbs us from morning onwards. When a person wants to visit us next morning at nine we agree. We know he is coming for his own work and he is visiting us to discuss his work. Yet we feel tension.

Here the need is his and not ours. Yet the night before we are restless. We doubt whether we would get up in time to receive him. We spend a restless night.

Our anxiety is to get up early. That means when someone or we ourselves direct our mind to do a particular thing by a particular time we are experiencing stress. This needs to be corrected.

At proper time proper tasks are done and they give good results. So one should stop worrying beforehand.

FATHER SHOULD BECOME GRAND FATHER

The child we see everyday at home will grow up and one day she will go to her in-laws. Then we are forced to see her only once a week.

Afterwards it becomes once a month. Later on we reason with ourselves whether we should go every month. Without our effort now the visits will become quarterly.

After a while they change into long telephonic conversations. "How are you, child? How is your health. Hope you have no problems.

"Do you get good sleep? Tell me, what more news? What have you cooked today. Do you get good vegetables there? Is milk of good quality?" This way we are concerned about every little thing.

This conversation which usually lasts for half an hour in the beginning comes down to five minutes because everyone feels this is a routine conversation serving no purpose and is a waste of money.

We feel upset at home when we don't see things at their proper place. Is it not painful not to see one's own daughter at home who added zing to life till now?

If we try to share our agony with others to find comfort they tend to retort, "Has not your wife left her home to be with you?" This is the problem of a sentimental fool, that is the father of a girl child.

Infact one needs two hearts one to feel happy that daughter is happy wherever she is and another to feel the pain of child's absence and separation.

SELECT ONLY AN EQUAL

When we are faced with problems and are upset we share our thoughts with a person who we think is our well wisher. But that person will almost conduct an inquiry and try to find fault with us. He makes use of this opportunity to prove himself as a great man.

We should keep this type of narrow-minded people at a distance. It is a mistake to consider them to be close to us.

If we seek the help of a mean person he thinks he is far superior and looks down on us.He will not solve our problem. We can find him exhibiting his ego but cannot find a way to solve our problems.

Helping a person in difficulties should become an immediate duty. When we visit a doctor, he should find out what ails us and take immediate measures. This is the true characteristic of a good doctor.

He should not blame the patient saying he himself was responsible for his disease. When the patient is cured the doctor can advise him what to do and what not to do. He should explain things to him so that he can realise his mistake. It is barbaric to make fun of the victim and torture him with words.

When we are surrounded by the problems our discretion diminishes to some extent. One lacks clarity to see the problems as they are. Even the smallest thing is magnified to frightening proportions.

At this time we need a few words of solace and proper advice. Sympathy may not solve a problem but it gives comfort thus lessening the intensity. When mind is peaceful even complex things can be easily resolved.

USE COLLOQUIAL TERMS

We get recognition in the world in many ways. Some people become popular because of family name. Some others are popular with their own name.Some people get recognition when both these things combine. Some other names are linked with their profession, organisation or status.

It is futile to keep all these things aside and to seek recognition for one's own self. This mentality will place others in difficulties.

Suppose a person by name Prasad visits our home when we are not there, our problem starts.There are several Prasads whom we know. We can't make out who this Prasad is. That is why we cannot ring him nor will we try to meet him.

Someone else phones us and proudly announces, "Iam Venkatrao." He will not clarify which Venkatrao he is. There are so many Venkatraos.

If we ask him for our own information, "Which Venkatrao?" He will be very angry."So you can't recognise me? True, you are a great man. How can you remember a person like me?" Why do they quiz us on the telephone, "Guess who I am?" Why should they think it is below their dignity to give their details on the phone.

We should adjust to all such small matters. We should be clear to make the other person understand. Our mentality and personality should be as clear as a glass, to the other person.

IF YOU HAVE NO CONTROL, DON'T MEDDLE

As there is a vast world in the ocean, so also human body is a world in itself with cells, nerves, muscles and a lot more machinery. That is why lakhs of cells die and lakhs of cells are born everyday. Actually these processes are not concerned with us.

The mother earth bears so much to help us walk. So also our body keeps so many things from us to help us continue with our life. We are not worried about some deluge that may occur one day. Similarly we need not worry about our body.

The ocean is not concerned with the world within.There are plants, animals and all types of beings. They too have conflicts and enmities.

But the ocean is busy with its own work.It looks peaceful. Except on occasions when storm rages, the ocean is peaceful always.

That is why we should also not worry about the various processes and changes that are taking place in the body. Without fear we should continue with our work. Then our life becomes comfortable. With no fear for life, we start liking ourselves.

Keeping aside the anxiety regarding body matters which we do not understand, if we turn our sight inward and develop optimism, our life will have a smooth running.

WORLD IS WIDE FOR THE UNINVITED

We have a mouth but we do not know how to talk appropriately. Either we are garrulous or dumb. There are some who are different. They talk frankly and whole heartedly. Those who express what they feel are better people than those who do measured talk.

I know a person who greets everyone he comes across and exchanges pleasantries. Even if we are busy talking to others he waits till we are through and then talks to us with great warmth.

Those who seek favour from us anyway wait for us to be free to talk about their problem. They don't leave us in peace till their work is done. But there are some others who do not have any selfish motive. They don't expect anything. They don't seek anything. We only feel the fragrance of their cordiality. What a great quality!

If we always make it a point that we respond to others only when they greet us first and try to pose as a person of serious demeanour we will be treated as outsiders. The one who makes a conscious effort to enquire others welfare and pleases himself reflects his heart in his words.

Mouth is there to utter good words. Ears are there to listen to good things. Eyes are there to see good around. If we strive for others well-being, our welfare will be taken care of by the lord of the universe. We give only a little to others but what we receive is enormous.

SEE YOURSELF WITHIN YOU

Even before starting a work we are full of anxiety whether we could do the work well or not, whether it could be finished in time or not. If we think and plan properly half the work is done. But we don't do it because of fear.

We have an inferiority complex that we are very low and small in stature. That is why we are not able to think well and do great things. But we are in no way inferior to anyone. We have adequate capabilities to face problems if there are any.

Then what is the use? Our fear is obstructing us from starting any work. Because of this fear our talent and creativity are on the wane. Outwardly we say "We don't have great ambitions." But these are mere words. In our heart of hearts we also want to do something and achieve something. Nothing wrong in it.

If we become blind the world becomes dark. Life becomes unbearable. But the mere fear that we may become blind is terrible. This fear is more tortuous than the blindness itself.

Is there any meaning to such crazy thoughts and fears? Is there any scientific attitude? We know the answer is "No." But we are captives of fear. We ourselves are inviting trouble.

A courageous man dies only once and a coward dies every day. With self confidence we can achieve anything. There is nothing we cannot get if we dare. No one is ruined because of bravery.

EACH ACCORDING TO HIS WILL

We like only some people.Of them, some we like more. Again we get closer to one person.

Since we like a few qualities in that person or a few of his methods, we may start adoring him. There is nothing wrong.

To love a person is one's independent choice. But we expect others also to accept this person whom we adore as a good and great person.

We want everyone to love, respect and adore that person. So whenever we get an opportunity we praise him, talk high of him and exaggerate. We almost exhibit a tendency bordering on,"If you don't admire that person, there must be something wrong with you." This blind admiration naturally annoys the other person.The person we admire may be great but because of our extremity, others will start disliking him.

This way we are harming the person indirectly. These extreme tendencies are applicable to gods also.

In the name of admiration, we are making that person an enemy to others. Love, respect and reverence are personal feelings. If we try to impose these an others, we will be doing more harm than good.

WE TOO HAVE LIGHT AND SHADE

We live with a strong belief that we are behaving correctly,very systematically and we are doing everything right. That is why if anyone says, "You are wrong", our anger knows no bounds. "Are you so great as to find fault with me?" we thunder. We don't understand that it is wrong to be so intolerant and so angry with others.

Infact, our acts should be acceptable to others. For that we have to regularly review ourselves. We should correct ourselves. Since we love ourselves most,we fail to see our faults.Even if a thought crosses our mind, "Perhaps it is not the right path", we delude ourselves.

We think that all others do wrong and we alone do right. We are harming ourselves by compromising thus.We don't realise that we should not praise ourselves but others should. We also develop a tendency not to listen to others. So we select a thorny path and face many difficulties.

We should have open mind. When someone shows our defects, whether they are elders or youngsters does not matter,we should correct ourselves.We cannot learn everything by experience. One life is not enough for that. So we have to listen to certain things and practise.We should consider the society around as a looking glass. We should not consider ourselves to be very handsome, by looking in the mirror.

This society is a thermometer to measure our mistakes.

PATIENCE MATTERS

We get everything as a result of our deeds. With that faith we can plan anything and implement the same with confidence.

When the results are favourable we think it is all due to our talent. As long as things are smooth there is no problem. If anything goes wrong and we have to face unforeseen problems we get panicky.

"Oh, how can I face them? How can I solve them?" are the doubts that surround us and upset us. We seek somebody's help and advice.

In fact when we are in trouble we don't accept anyone's advice. Not that the other person is not giving us right advice, but we don't listen to him. Thus we seek advice from many but do not follow any. This leads to more complications.

We can see everything clearly if it is someone else's problem. Why is it so? Because we do not have any bias or predetermined views. So we understand everything clearly. When it comes to us our problems start. In many cases it is better to continue with our work. But sometimes it is beneficial not to take any action.

Instead of worrying ourselves to death thinking how to solve problems it is better to stop thinking so that one may have peace.

When one is in a thoughtless state there are no bonds. We should not forget the truth that our problems are born out of attachments.

ONE CANNOT EAT WHILE SERVING

Anyone can do only one thing at a time. No one can do several things simultaneously. Even if someone plans to do so, they will not be comprehensive and certainly lack some thing. There cannot be success.

Even in the case of money, all are not capable of spending. Especially a person who works hard to earn money cannot enjoy by spending it.

What he knows and does is work itself. He continues to work but the thought that he can enjoy the fruits of his work does not cross his mind.

He very much wants his own people should get comfort and happiness with his money.He thinks that his money should be enjoyed by his people thus making his hard work rewarded.

His family members point of view is somewhat different.

People hesitate to spend money earned by someone else. Even wife and children hesitate thinking they may be spending excessively. They fear the person who is working hard to earn money since they recognise the value of money that was earned in a hard way.

But the head of the family will be happy if they can spend moderately without going to extremes because he himself is not inclined to spend any money on himself.

It is difficult to spend the hard earned money the same way it is hard for a sensitive heart to offend others.

THE SPECTACLES SHOULD NOT BE OBSTRUCTING

Usually we get endless flow of thoughts. Unstable mind runs in many directions. One problem can have many solutions. We should select only a convenient one to get the best solution.

We should not be undecided about what should be done. By nature we are a confused lot, always in chaos. In addition if our mind too fails us our life will be full of entanglements. The root cause of all this is lack of clarity within us.

So the world does not know what type we are, what type of reactions we have and what we do when.

If we are unstable in our behaviour we are left with no value in society. Besides we have to face criticism. Others think it is only inviting trouble to have any dealings with us because of our unpredictability in every thing. Every one loses faith in us.

If we can understand ourselves and if our views and feelings are stable that does a world of good for us as well as others. They try to understand and adjust to our nature. In case they don't like our attitude, they just leave us. It is also good in a certain way.

There is no such thing as everyone will be liked by everyone else. Yet we will be lonely if no one understands us. Our face should reflect our personality.

DONATE SERVICE

While looking after our own affairs and shouldering the responsibilities of the family,we would like to do something for the society and people. It is good to have selfless thoughts along with selfish thoughts.

To help others, and to be useful to others within our capacity is indeed a fortune. But we should not trouble anyone just because we are doing good to someone. We should remember this is only for our own happiness.

We should do whatever we do with our own capability. It is enough if we could do to the extent possible. "I am doing service. So, you please help me", sounds ridiculous.There are many who cheat the people in the name of service. Now the meaning of service has completely changed.

On the contrary, if we do whatever service humbly and honestly, we will have hundreds of people with us. There is no need to have an organisation or a society for this. It is mad to think of a position. It is not only that an organisation or a position in an organisation is not needed to support your service mindedness but also they prove to be a hindrance at times for your wider scope of activities. There is happiness in seeking everybody's comfort. A person with such great mentality will himself turn to be a great force to shape this system it self.

ALL ARE YOUR PEOPLE

We talk big and declare great ideals. We say all religions are equal. People and their hearts are important, there is no use of caste and creed, we assert. If anyone questions us what our caste is,we look down on him.All these are outward things and thorough lies.In our offices, factories, organisations, politics and even in hermitages, we engage our own people.We consider their welfare to be of utmost importance.We form societies and remain united.

If anyone questions,"Why your friends, your office staff, your admirers, and whom you admire are all your people?", you will justify, "Yes, our methods, our thoughts, our customs are alike. So we are able to stay united.That is why we are able to achieve progress."

We are happy to be ditched by our own people. We don't have discernment to know who is good and who is bad. Even if the other person speaks truth, we say they are wrong. We give permits, promotions, increments to our own people or recommend these things for them. With this narrow-mindedness we are burying eligible and good hearted people.

We should be united not in the name of religious faiths or castes.Humanity and broadmindedness should be our nature.

If this is lacking, one is lowly irrespective of the high positions they occupy. Those who look at everyone equally without taking into account colour, looks, caste or creed are indeed great people.

FOR ACTION REPETITION IS NO FALLACY

Without our knowledge, without our concern at times we feel depressed. We wonder why we are spending the days the same way, doing the same thing everyday.

We whine saying that life is rotating like a wheel. Dawn and dusk, the same routine work and beyond that there is nothing new.

We think it will be a challenge to take up a new task and we will have enthusiasm to go forward. We forget the fact that for human existence and for community life every task and every profession are important.

Though we know each one has a particular place in society and without whom and without their work the society misses something we tend to look down on ourselves.

Lack of self-esteem disturbs our mental peace. We should realise our own importance. Our presence and our duty should be always with us.

We know how immensely the billions of living things in this creation are benefited by the sun and the moon who never go astray from their path.

Similarly even though our daily routine is the same we should feel creativity and progress in every dawn.

We are not averse to the food we consume everyday. We don't stop sleeping because it is everyday occurence.

To think that our daily work is routine and boring is like asking our heart to stop beating because it has done that for long.

WE CAN ONLY SHOW THE WAY

We are eager to share what we know and help others as far as possible. Others are willing to accept the help because it mitigates their suffering and gives them comfort.

Similarly we want tell our own people whatever we know and try to correct them whenever they go wrong. But they are not ready for this. Without any selfish motive we want to correct them. Not only they do not agree with us but they also rebel.

"Are you such a great person as to advise us? Don't we know this much? Even otherwise our way is ours. We know what is good or what is bad for us. Stop this unnecessary interference," they say with vehemence.

Anyway we cannot be concerned about everyone in this world. We think it is our duty to help our friends at least. Friends naturally influence each other. Both are benefited because of the friendship.

But friendship between two different mentalities may not last long. In such cases it is difficult to reform even friends.

A person who seeks warm friendship has to be alone. Or he should have a great loving heart to love the whole world while effacing himself. Common people like us cannot have such noble qualities as to give up our ego.

It is essential to follow limits in everything. One should not go too deep into matters even with a view of reforming others.

SEE WITH MY EYES

We think we are very good people. We also believe that there can be no better person than us. Every human being has good as well as bad qualities. But people tend to look only at their goodness. They don't see bad side. Doesn't everyone look beautiful in front of a looking glass?

Any wellwisher of ours may analyse our character and tell us about ourselves, that certain thoughts of ours are really good, but there is a kind of behaviour which is not good and if we correct ourselves we can become a complete person with good qualities.

When he says good things about ourselves we are very happy. When he mentions our bad qualities we don't relish it. Besides we think he is misunderstanding us. So we start arguing. We don't even hesitate to have a conflict with him saying, "I am correct. Suppose I follow your advice it may harm me."

We don't really want to neglect his advice. Every one would like to correct oneself. But we don't consider anything wrong with ourselves. In a way our explanation is not wrong.

This world is understood by every one differently. Though the object is same depending on the point of view of a person it looks different. No one does it consciously. What they know is their world. No one agrees in this world to call himself a bad person.

SOME FLOWERS DON'T FRUCTIFY

We enjoy showering pity and saying sympathetic words. All right, having done this, are we going to help them any way? No. Not at all.

These are only words. So we are liberal with them. "Poor fellow, he does not have a job. This one has no education at all. Those people can't make both ends meet. This man is always ill." All these kind words result in nothing.

Especially this sympathy is too much towards childless couples. They know it is not in anybody's hands. This is a natural thing. Yet they persist, "You don't have children, you don't get children." They don't care how these words hurt others.

First, childless couples feel sorry they don't have children. Then they will grieve.They try every means that is humanly possible. When there is no results, they come to a conclusion that they cannot become parents in this life.

"All those who love us are our children. Let us look after their welfare.There is happiness in that.It is meaningful to look after the children of others as our own." With this satisfaction, they continue with their life.

Is it right to look down on such couples and to show sympathy? All are not equipped with every thing.There are some plusses and there are some minuses. Even we have some and we don't have some others.

It is a great mistake to show sympathy for others and to think that it is our great qualification.

"NO" DOES NOT MEAN COWARDICE

For ages there are a few traditions, principles and prohibitions in our life stream. All these have been scientifically thought about and determined by ancestors.

We don't listen to anything that is told directly. We ask for logic behind it. Though there are answers for everything, when it leads to argument, practice becomes nil.

We are advised to take our meals after cleaning our feet and hands.If parts are not washed, then there will be poverty and misery. This is all very blunt.

But the real idea is to motivate us to keep ourselves clean. Frightening is not their idea at all. They feel that if we are not frightened, we may be carefree and lead a bad life.

For festivals and celebrations, we are advised to have buntings of mango leaves. This is a precaution taken to clear the air of bacteria when people gather in crowds. So also recommending fast on a particular day is aimed at keeping us mentally and physically fit.

Without taking all these things into consideration, we think these are all meaningless customs which take us backwards. Infact these are all good traditions for the welfare of human beings.

A person with pure mind and body can do anything.He can fearlessly accomplish any difficult task with ease. The aim of our life is to live fearlessly.

YOU AND HE ARE THE SAME

There is a difference in physical appearance between persons. When it comes to attitudes and mentalities there is a lot more difference. For coexistence these differences do not become obstacles.

We all are living harmoniously in the society. The difficulty arises when everyone keeps his opinion to himself.

Communication gap leads to many misunderstandings and mishaps. When we come to know someone made an adverse remark about us, and if that someone happens to be our friend, we should ask the concerned person frankly to know the truth. If that person is an outsider who sullied our name we should not take him into account.

When a word travels from person to person many things are added.

In what context, in what conversation the original statement is made goes into oblivion. When taken out of context that statement may sound wrong.

So we are upset. We nourish this misunderstanding and let it grow. Suppose the other person had really said something like that, whatever happened to our understanding of him till now? Has all the past along with his goodness vanished? This should not happen that way.

We should get out of the meanness of misunderstanding.

THERE ARE PERMANENT THINGS IN TEMPORARY

First, we should select a task which is according to our liking and taste. Then we should continue to work in that area. We should achieve success. If not, the most valuable time in life is wasted.

For example, here is an incident. One boss tells his subordinate, "You know this organisation. You know discipline.For the last ten years, you are working here. Knowing the practice prevalent in this office you are going in the wrong direction. Do you know what is the punishment for this?"

"Yes sir, I know. Either you give a memo or suspend me. But there is no need for either because here is my resignation. I know there will be a need for this one day. That is why I carry it in my pocket. Good bye to your methods, your office and your discipline." And he walks out with great show.

What we can't understand here is, why did that man carry that resignation letter in his pocket for the last ten years and also continued to work. He should have left the place in the beginning itself.

We can understand only one thing. He is only an opportunist. He stayed there till it was necessary for him. Once it is over, he harangued and left.

There is one thing which is better than carrying a resignation letter in the pocket. One day, it can be any day or any moment, we all have to leave this world. For that we all should be ready. This is what is called being brave.

WE SHOULD EXPERIENCE WHAT WE CANNOT GET BACK

Our minds are always agitated and filled with anxieties. That is why we like to be silent. Children's minds are peaceful and clear. That is why they like noise very much.

When we are not in a good mood,we chide children.This is our mistake, not the mistake of the children.It is not nice to see children being silent and behaving like elders. Similarly if elders behave like children, it does not befit them.It is not a good method to chide children showing off our grown up status. It is pleasant to see children play with toys, to make noise or even to break things.

When young people hop or run, it is a pleasant sight. If elderly people do the same, it looks awkward. That is why one should act according to the age. There is beauty as well as happiness in that.

When it comes to desires also, elders should not have children's desires and children should not have elder's desires.

Even dress has to suit the profession and status. Only children can comfort us in our worries and anxieties. For that at least we should embrace them and play with them. We should be one among them. The happiness we get out of it defies analysis.

If we look back, we also were mischievous as children. But we forget that and restrict children from play and mischief. Our mental and physical health is supposed to be good only when we can play with children and are able to bear their noise.

DON'T SEARCH FOR AN EXCUSE

Whatever we may say, however we may proclaim, it is a fact that we live in this material world. There is no point in giving up mundane things and daily necessities.

In the name of self-respect we only exhibit our ego. We can't stand any adverse comment. We react ferociously saying, "I can't tolerate such words. I cannot kill my own personality." This attitude is affecting the wife and children who are depending on us.

Whom does this so called self-respect help? Who is pleased with this? One should think before taking any action. One should remember the welfare of the wife and children. One should question oneself, "What about them? What will happen to them if I take an action like this?"

When we have a suitable answers for the above questions we should proceed further with the decision taken. If we overreact saying "My self-respect is offended," others start pitying us. Those who are obsessed with themselves only talk of self-respect every now and then.

One should not take decisions in a moment of emotion. That will cause permanent damages. In fact, a person with self-respect has immense patience as well. He is a man of courage. He lives in reality.

A person who has not gone wrong hardly thinks of self-respect. A person without any flaw always holds his head high even when others point their fingers at him.

Is it self-respect to give up one and to seek favour from another? If it is a must one may change one's route but not the goal.

HARD WORK SHOULD BE OURS

If we do not spend money we call it thrift. If the other person does the same we call it miserliness. Some would rather die than spend money. There are others who spend lavishly.We think we are lucky if we come across a person of gentle nature who is charitably inclined.

Now we take over the right of his money. We appeal to his sentiments and extract money from him. For any reason if he refuses to give money as much as we expected we are very much upset.

We say harsh things as if we kept our money with him. We give wide publicity how stingy he is about money. We also abuse him. "He has so much money. Would he die if he helps me. What would he do with all his money?"

We behave without any common sense that we have no right over his money.

Suppose we were in his place would we have given away as much money as the other person demanded. Why so far? We see so many who are not as fortunate as we are. But are we helping them within our own limits? The answer is no.

We ourselves are not doing what we can and what we should. On our part we expect the other person to do what we want him to do.

We are not born to exploit others. Good or bad, gain or loss we have to be on our own. That is what we call independent life.

RECTIFYING MISTAKES

We try to imitate others ever since our childhood. First we imitate our parents. We would love to become like them, to talk like them and behave like them. We feel proud of it. But when we grow up we realise that this imitation is wrong.

We understand that we should think independently and we should have our own personality to have our place in this society. At the same time we also inherit some traits from our parents.

We may inherit or we may not inherit wealth or property but we certainly inherit good and bad traits from our fore fathers. It is fine to have good traits but when we have bad traits we have to face the music.

We also inherit physical diseases. Should we accuse our parents for that?

There are many medicines to control physical ills. So there is nothing to worry on that account.

But we should guard against bad traits and see that they are corrected by our effort. We should make use of our education and culture to remove bad tendencies that come on their own.

We are not responsible for our birth. But we are responsible for our mind. A person who consciously moulds his life in the right way for happy life alone is successful.

DON'T TIE YOURSELF IN KNOTS

Normally, we do a lot of thinking. If they are happy thoughts, it is nice. But mostly frightening and painful thoughts come to us frequently. Our people are somewhere in a far off town. Our children go somewhere for education. We think of them and their welfare. We doubt if they are all right. We imagine all sorts of things and get frightened.

Suppose, we go out of town leaving sick mother, father, boy or girl behind. We go out of compulsion. Having gone there, we feel very restless. We have no peace of mind. If there is no way to contact them on the phone, there is no end to frightening thoughts.

Why that far? We are hesitant even to visit a friend or a relative who is admitted in hospital. We don't know in what state he is. Can we withstand that? This is all due to our love for others. When we actually see, things may not be as bad as we imagined. It is always easy to confront a situation practically than to torture ourselves with imaginary fears.

We will come to know of the news whether it is good or bad.But we imagine only bad and get depressed. We get worried that we have not heard anything. But no news is good news.

FIRST OR NEXT DOES NOT MATTER

In marriages and celebrations, we come across relatives and friends. There is a problem there. We don't know who should greet first.Infact, it does not matter. Whoever may greet, we reciprocate. So also others respond to our greeting.

If we miss greeting, then the relatives will distance themselves. That will gradually turn into enmity. One will not stand the other. They talk ill of each other. They say these people are proud. These people will say they are arrogant. This will lead to more complications.

To avoid all this whether a person is big or small, woman or man, we ourselves should take initiative and greet them. They will happily respond. If there is any odd one who does not respond because of arrogance, leave him alone. Discard him. It is in our hands. On the contrary,if we form an opinion beforehand about others, then there will be a lot of troubles.

We don't become small by greeting first. Our status will increase and will not come down by that. Good person can never be bad.

So if our mind is clear, we need not worry what the other person thinks of us. Forgetting the differences, limitations of age and obstacles of status, if we treat everyone as our own selves and mix well, the happiness we get out of it is something wonderful.

DON'T BITE OFF MORE THAN YOU CAN CHEW

We continue to be working for something or the other. We always work hard either mentally or physically. It is a good thing to be ever working. But if we continuously pressurize mind and body,they will rebel. They stop working and seek asylum from doctors. So some rest is needed.When our mind is tired,we should cooperate by not thinking. When our limbs refuse to work, we sholuld reduce physical labour to allow them to recover. Craving for something, with anxiety for achievement we are mercilessly commanding our body and limbs. We are hard towards them and make them work.It is not correct.

I recently met a gentleman. He is eighty years old. He has written many books. He has studied a lot.He is a treasure-house of knowledge. Earlier, one of his eyes was affected.

Now he lost sight in the second eye also. He is totally blind. Since he is a greatman, famous eye surgeons came to him and told that they would operate on his eye and try to get back his sight.They requested him to agree to this. He politely declined. He says,"My eyes studied several books from my childhood and they helped me write several books. They have seen all the important things in the world.I gave them a lot of trouble. They want to rest now and are not functioning. So I do not want to disturb them."

I realised what a stoic he is and how equanimous!

NATURALLY WE ARE ALL GOOD

If we get any favour from anyone, we feel very embarrassed. Suppose we are travelling in the train and fellow traveller orders coffee for us without consulting us, we are obliged.

That small thing will do. We are under obligation. As long as he talks we should also talk. If he goes out saying, "Please attend to my luggage", we have to keep an eye on that.

I don't say it is wrong. But because we had coffee at his expense, we have to shoulder many responsibilities.Not that we cannot buy our coffee. Even his idea was not to cause us inconvenience. Just for fun, as a fellow traveller he offers us coffee. But if we get any help from anybody, till we repay we become his slave. This is a good quality. Gratitude is golden.

Some people run enthusiastically for free coffee and meals. They grab as much as they can. We come across many such people. They spend days forever searching easy targets.

They don't have any scruples as we mentioned earlier. They accept anything happily and forget the good we have done the very moment.

Forgetfulness is a great boon to them. Man is not alone. Life is not "touch me not."We should get from some and distribute among all.

BE KIND TO YOURSELF

We become weak when we emotionally depend on others. They tend to exploit us. They think without them we cannot survive. They rub off their mistakes on us. This is worse than bonded labour. More unbearable than a body without back bone. This total dependence is a slavery worse than all weaknesses.

The only mistake we have committed is to love in excess. Now that love itself becomes a crime. So we get punished by those whom we love. Why all this trouble? Why can't we divert that swelling love towards ourselves to live happily and peacefully.

When we are physically weak we depend on medicine. When we have financial needs we depend on the person who lends the money. Everyone faces these troubles at some time or the other.

But we overcome them. If we depend on others mentally no one comes to our rescue. This problem is to be sorted out by ourselves.

When our conscience is clear we need not bother about others. Real love is when there is mutual understanding and need for each other. That lasts for ever and is a comfort to both.

If it is one way traffic one is doomed. We may wait for the other person, but can never make the other person wait for us. We should desire others only as much as they desire us. If we show excess love they will throw us out. When those for whom we long do not care for us what should we do–Just leave it.

LET US SELECT ONLY GOOD WORDS

When we want to say a thing to others, we are careful enough not to use harsh words and not to hurt them. What we want to say, the other person knows. Even we know. All those listening to us also know. Because of culture, we talk courteously and softly but there is no difference in subject or in effect.

There is nothing more we gain by saying the same thing roughly, bluntly and directly. Moreover we would have hurt the other person. Our words will pierce like a thorn.

It is not at all wrong to talk without hurting. The word that is said without offending both is the best method. We don't want to cause inconvenience to others. We don't want to hurt them also. That is why we sometimes hesitate to tell the truth. At last we tell them somehow. In the meantime, we struggle with ourselves how to tell.

When we come to the conclusion that there is no other way except this and there is no other solution, it is better to tell the truth without hiding anything. We do not intend to harm them.There is no cheating involved either. Only thing is that there is a difference between what we thought first and how we told them later.

We have come to this conclusion because of the circumstances. It will benefit both. Since there is no fault in our thought and decision, it is good for both. It is certain.

LET THERE BE NO METAMORPHOSIS

We always want things we like. They should be with us and they should belong to us. We don't want things we don't like. They should not be anywhere near us. This is how our desires move.

We want flowers but not the thorns. We want comforts but not hardships. We should live for ever. Death should never approach us.

Our thoughts always hover over others and we always compare ourselves with others.We want whatever they have. If they don't have, we need not have. How can it be? Should everyone have everything?

If one does physical labour, he has good health. Physical labour is his livelihood. The man who moves in cars has no opportunity to have a full meal or to have a sound sleep.

In his life, every minute is ridden with problems. His daily routine is not to be caught by these problems.

Now who is more fortunate, the one who is poor or the millionaire? Each one thinks the other one is more fortunate.

The rich man is not ready to accept poverty. The ordinary man living with mental peace is not ready to accept disturbed mind.

Infact, we know all these things. We should work hard for gaining something.We should not live in perpetual worry for something or the other. Each one has his life and each one has his death. Each one has his life and each one has his happiness.There is no comparison between one man and the other in this world.

TASTE THE FRUIT OF SUCCESS

Every person is concerned about his future. Leaving aside disappointment and pessimism he is moving ahead charged with hope and ambition.

Today no one is indulging in comparing oneself with someone else thus wallowing in sorrow or happiness. Every one has one's own life to lead. One has taken control of one's own growth.

Nowadays when there are many social changes that are taking place no one is looking around to compare oneself with another to know where one stands on the ladder of success.

Every person is growing within his scope. All are absorbing success equally. Earlier rarely a person used to be successful whereas others were content with ordinary lives. Today all have equal opportunities.

All are making good use of these opportunities. A large number of them are succeeding. Education and knowledge are growing.

All parents want to give good education to their children and make all efforts in this direction. So it is wrong to think someone is envious of us since all are tasting success.

Ours are independent lives. We have our goals and we make every effort to reach that goal.

The truth that our success depends on our effort should guide us towards our goal.

MANY IN ONE

Wishing that all should be happy, people say, **Sarve Jana Sukhinobhavanthu.** They declare their broad-mindedness and say, "I am a world citizen." There is indeed greatness in thinking the whole world is mine and each one in this world belongs to me. Only great personalities show this in deeds and not in words. We salute them and remember them first thing in the morning.

One of my friends prays to God,"Protect me alone, Venkatachalapathi." Once I asked him, "What is this? You so selfishly pray for your own protection."

Then he explained, "See, if I am all right, my wife is all right. My children will be all right. So if he protects me. He is protecting my family. Moreover we should not read out a long list before God. He may get irritated. It is enough if everyone prays for his own welfare."

One way it is true. To some extent there is selfishness and hope in praying for himself and his family members through him. Beyond that, if he represents everyone around him and asks for their protection that shows more selfishness and greed.

If we stand like a lamp, the light spreads around. All our people will be safe in that light. That way one light for a family is enough. The pained world will be filled with light and there will be happiness and comfort. Individual progress belongs to collectivity. Individual development becomes an enlightened path to society.

DARKNESS AND LIGHT ARE NOT TWO DIFFERENT THINGS

"If delayed, manna may turn into poison," said elders. They also said,"It is important to be slow." Does it mean these two statements are contradicting each other? Contradictory? Not at all. Both are correct.

In this world, each thing has two sides. Even if they look contrary to each other, both the statements are true.They are to be applied according to the context. In one context if it is said, "There is nothing better than silence. Unnecessary talk leads to misery", in some other context one has to say,"Without expressing what is there in one's mind, not uttering a word and doing all the evil that is possible, silently, is not good." These statements are not contradicting each other.

Not only that. The same person can talk differently on different occasions. These two may be quite contradicting each other. One should not conclude that he uses, "Double speak" and he has no stability. Each matter has two extremes. Whichever side one inclines, one loses balance. If one understands both sides, it will be clear how to strike balance.The proper life style implies one has to understand this suitable balance.

There are all types of truths. What should be accepted,to what extent and when, should depend upon our experience and circumstances.

We may listen to a number of things, we may read very many things, yet while applying them, we have to have our own knowledge and clear context.

IF YOU SUPPRESS IT BECOMES AN ATOM BOMB

If we like a thing we do not know where to stop. Without caring for health we gobble down everything. Every day we drink tea and coffee. We go to movies. We go out for picnics. We organise parties and enjoy.

This way we always satisfy our wants. Sometimes we get angry with others. Sometimes we express our love. This way we are known to the world by our habits and actions. As a result some people appreciate us. Some others find fault with us.

Be it as it may, it is comfortable to be ourselves. It is better to be in our own dreamy world, facing petty little problems that make life thrilling instead of struggling to be known as a good person or undergoing rigours to be a healthy person.

It is not for human beings to live mechanically and routinely as if cast in a mould. That is why they say a human being should not become a machine. We are not able to look separately at a person's habits and his attitudes.

A person's habits are limited to himself whereas his attitudes have effect on others. A person with bad habits in the view of society need not be judged as a bad person.

There is no relationship between intellect and weaknesses. Personal weaknesses need not be given importance. It is important to know what he is doing for the society, and how he is conducting himself.

People with minor vices may be trusted. If someone is viewed as a person without any bad habit one should be cautious because if one has no minor vices he is sure to have major vices.

SHOULD SELECT ONLY GOOD

"Do some exercise atleast for five minutes in a day" says the doctor. "Remember God atleast for five minutes in a day" says the spiritualist.

"Meditate for five minutes in a day. You will get inner happiness" says yoga expert. The psychologist says, "Five minutes are enough. You review your good and bad deeds. You can become a great person in life."

The dental surgeon says, "Take care of your teeth just for five minutes. Your ill health will disappear." A person practising Naturopathy says, "Have a nice bath for five minutes. That will free you from diseases." When everyone advises about five minutes we do not know what to do.

All these are good but can we practise them? We do not have the opportunity to do them all nor do we have time to do so.

Ultimately we end up doing nothing thus wasting our time. There are many things that are beneficial to us. All these are told by elders for our own good. But we cannot practise them all because we have to do many other things for a living.

In this world each one has his own lifestyle. It is enough if one can practise what is possible within one's limits. They can be happy and comfortable.

We should give up the anxiety that we are not able to practise everything. If we do what we know keeping in mind our priorities we can accomplish everything.

SILENCE FRIGHTENS

Though fear and courage are two different characteristics, there is a close relationship between them. We should know what is courage and what is fear. If we mistake one for the other, results will be topsy-turvy.

"What happened exactly? Why did you do like that, tell me," we ask. But the other person will not utter a word. It is not a police station. It is not a court room. It is our house and it is our family matter. We want to know the truth so that we can find a solution to the problem. But the other person does not speak. He stands there stubbornly without uttering a word.

If we resort to punishment, the reply is, "I am afraid." Actually it was not fear. It is obstinacy. "Why should I reply?" is the attitude.

In the name of cowardice, he undertakes adventure, exhibits fearlessness and calls it fear.

One does not speak out when one is determined. The one who gets easily frightened speaks out every word. If any one says, "Because of fear, or cowardice or fearing some harm, I dared not tell you the truth," it is to be understood that it is an utter lie.

If one does not know facts, situation could be grave. Then no way is left except punishment.

If one does not speak out truth, in spite of persuasion and pleading, we have to consider him as a dare devil.

WE ARE GETTING USED TO THIS!

There are lakhs of problems in the society around us. Besides the bad traditions continuing for generations, many more problems are emerging because of growing bad habits, immorality, cheating and fraud.

But the society is also getting used to some problems. It does not mean they are no more problems.One should not have indifference to an old problem.

If the society has compromised as it could not face the problem, it does not mean it no longer remains a problem and the society has accepted it.

For example, smoking and drinking are common things now. Dowry giving and accepting are going on without hindrance.

We are not in a position to consider these things as problems. We are not thinking that we are facing a problem.

Accepting graft,telling lies, cheating... all are becoming common. If any one mentions these, we have come to a state to express, "Is it a big thing?"

They don't even have news value now.

This 'bad' which has become part of daily life should not be considered as accepted.

"We are used to this" is only a compromise. "It has become compulsory" is a weakness that should be removed.

Then only we can face these chronic problems.

HOW CAN YOU CLOSE THE MIND?

We love, love and love. But the person whom we love gets disgusted. Our excessive love itself is the cause of this disgust. So they say, "Go, just go away." We can't imagine that love can be a crime.

We think everything else has limits but not love. So our love swells and drowns the other person as flood. They migrate to escape the impact of this flood. At the end we remain villains.

During the showers of our love only everything grew and prospered. When it became flood they started running away. "You better remain as rain. Who gave you the right to become a flood to drown me?" they say. But when there is rain will flood be far behind?

They say, "It is all right not to have your love instead of having your excessive love." But we are filled with love unlimited. If we ask it to vanish, will it vanish?

We sit on the sea shore and relax. We own the treasures of the sea. We conduct trade by sailing on the sea. Though the sea is useful to us in many ways, it can also create storms. Then there is turmoil in human life.

We want the sea but not the storms it creates. How is it possible? What is the way?

The sea has its own boundary and is kind enough not to cross it. What about us? Within a second our mind can reach the far end of universe. Our mind is deeper than the sea, endless and wonderful.

There is no argument in love.

WE, WHO HAVE GIVEN BIRTH TO THEM

Ideas and problems of today's youth is a big subject.

In general we comment, "Today's children are getting spoiled. They are not listening to their elders."

We expect our children to listen to us, do what we want them to do and study what we want them to study.

We also command them.

This is wrong.Did we do what our parents wanted us to do? Did we follow the path shown by them?

It is natural for a person to change according to times. We did the same.Our children will also change according to time.

We should understand the differences between generations. Even if they are our own children, they too have their individuality. They may be different from us. It does not mean they are distanced from our feelings.

As parents if we are good, children will definitely understand this and follow us.

Our day to day behaviour gives them guidance.

We should understand that our children are more intelligent than ourselves. We should put an end to commanding them. We should give them opportunities to think freely, independently and decide.

We should agree with what our children want to study, what they want to do and what path they want to choose and bless them.

DAILY WORK IS THE REALITY

Some of us are in job. We don't have satisfaction in that. We want to do better things because we think we are capable and we get depressed. Because of this,we cannot show interest in the present job and may face the danger of losing it.

Similarly, some of us start some business. We are ambitious to earn great profits in the beginning itself. Forgetting that we can improve by hard work, we start neglecting present business. Then we get into the mire of debts. When nothing is in our hand, we regret.

We should concentrate fully on the job we are doing and develop. If we start worrying about the present state and are always dissatisfied, we may lose even the present one.

We don't know the value of a thing when we have it.

Though we have money and status,we don't help fellow beings. When we lose power, we are eager to help others. We don't particularly care for a person who loves us and is with us. When we lose that person, we yearn for his love.

When we have eyes, we don't recognise their importance. When we grow blind, we cry for eyesight. In that state, no purpose will be served by these ideas.

We should be careful to see things as they are and to pay attention to them.

PAIN WILL BE PLEASURE

We always undergo some pain or the other. We want to escape that. We reach someone for consolation.

Life is an abode of pain and pleasure. There is no one who lives totally in grief or totally in happiness.

When we are confronted with a big difficulty, to have comfort we search for those who had withstood bigger problems. We don't search for a solution to our own problem.

Just as we feel natural to have comfort so also we should accept pain as part of life. Instead of facing the difficult situation, viewing it under a magnifying glass and grieving that we are confronted with the biggest problem will not help.

It is said, "Don't grieve that you lost a leg. Be happy that you have not lost your eye". But can a man who is grieving over his loss be happy about the thing he has not lost. How can one he happy in sorrow? Does that mean that we have to be unhappy while one is happy? So happiness is happiness and sorrow is sorrow. We should be ready for both.

We can't experience the eating of a fruit just by listening to its description however skillfully it might have been narrated. We experience its taste when we actually eat it. Similarly soothing words alone will not remove our pain. It is alleviated only when we experience it.

When we eat neem, gradually it tastes sweet. The distance will be reduced as we walk. As we bear the pain, so much pleasurable it will get.

WE DO WHILE LAUGHING, EXPERIENCE WHILE CRYING

We do mistakes knowingly or unknowingly. We are forgiven. But for crimes, whether they are committed knowingly or unknowingly, we get punishment.

Sometimes we may be punished for the crime we have not committed. It may be temporary and will pass.

We make fun of the person who is defeated. We are proud that we alone are great. We don't realise that defeat and victory are common and we also face them.

It is said one is freed of sin if confessed. May be it is true but committing sin and then confessing should not be a regular practice.

We want to earn money somehow. But it gives us mental peace only when we earn it in the right way.

We know what is not right.

We know what sin is.Yet we keep them aside when necessary.But can we escape their bad effects? No.

Since there are no lasting comfort and peace when one earns money unjustly and wrongly, some find lasting peace with a little money which they earn justly. That is the greatness of good.

We want to enjoy comforts but we are hesitant because of disease.

This hesitation should be there when we intend to harm others.

That is why it does not matter if we don't do good to others. Atleast we should not do harm.

JOSTLING LEADS TO SURE FALL

We often think that we don't get anything easily whereas others get it with ease. But if we achieve something with hardwork and diligence that will be lasting. The one that comes freely with ease will go away that easily.

If everyone in this world shoulders his responsibility well then there is no need for one to preach and another to listen. The differentiation between high and low will vanish. Every work and every individual will be respected. We understand that all are necessary in the society, all are respectable and all jobs are dignified. Then the system of single income and ten dependants will also disappear.

For some people it is easy to give work to others. But it is difficult for them to do work themselves.

When a person is not used to do work, even taking the trouble of eating one's own dinner becomes a drudgery. One has to eat to live. For eating one should work. By work only one can earn. So let us work.

When all members of the family work collectively their family will prosper. Then town, district, state, country and the whole world would be an ideal place to live.

For that good thoughts are required. Duty should be given importance. It is better to make it a practical reality.

The past is like a person who is no more. The future is like a child to be born. So we can do nothing about these things by worrying. That is why the present is of utmost importance. "I can do anything but I do not want to get out of this room" is no ideal to emulate.

LIST OF MISTAKES SHOULD BE SHORT

Ever since we get up in the morning, we commit many mistakes. There is nothing wrong. It is no surprise and it is not unnatural.

But we don't like to admit mistakes. Even when our conscience says we are wrong, we bluff, "I am not wrong. I didn't commit the mistake." To maintain one lie, we may have to tell hundred lies.

To cover up one mistake, we have to commit a hundred mistakes.

We think the other person will look down on us if we admit our mistake. We suspect he may blame us or punish us. Thus we imagine all sorts of things and get scared.

This mentality of not admitting one's mistake will ruin us in many ways. We may temporarily feel happy that we cheated the other person, but we don't progress any more.

Sometimes we don't know what the mistake is. When the other person points it out, one should admit it.

It is harmful to argue obstinately, "What mistake have I committed? What I did is correct." We should correct our mistakes instead of justifying them.

If we cover our mistake, even the other person will cover his mistake and cheat us. This way each one cheats the other one at the cost of good relations. Admitting one's mistake without hesitation reflects one's honesty.

EVERY PERSON IS SUCCESSFUL

We are exactly at a place where we fit. But we think we don't have the thing we have. We want to have a thing we don't have. This feeling is causing dissatisfaction among us. This dissatisfaction is an obstacle for our tomorrow. We can achieve what we want only when we march forward with satisfaction.

Just like balanced diet, we have pains and pleasures, gains and losses, ups and downs which we can bear and are good for us. We are worried because we don't realise this truth. We underestimate ourselves and torture ourselves. All this complication is an outcome of using money as the measuring scale, to determine a person's status.

Each one in society has a special place. No one is lower or no one is higher.

The place we got is a clean one.Naturally, we are equipped to safeguard this place. Sometimes we think someone is fortunate and someone is not but each one is happy in his own place. Even if one loses it temporarily, each one has power enough to regain it.

If our situation and status are not good, if only the one above has a right place, it means we cannot stay where we are. But we are safe as we are. That means the place is suitable to us. This is not compromising. Satisfaction does not mean compromise. It means to recognise the happiness we have, experience it and enjoy it.

DISTANCE IN MINDS

Now a days, human relations are becoming very delicate. They remind us of a proverb, 'losing one's nose by sneezing.'

When we want to have good relations like friendship, love, closeness and tenderness and want to continue with these relations, we are for ever feeling a certain insecurity.

We may be together for very long. But with one difference of opinion in a small matter, we separate. Today's closeness is becoming tomorrow's enmity.

Suppose there is a difference of opinion with our own people and start living separately, there is a need to be united, if necessary.This is the right principle.

For example, when we are celebrating an auspicious occasion, we have to invite those who had been our friends at one time though now they are enemies. So also forgetting everything else we should accept their invitation when they invite us. We should dismiss reservation and come forward to work for that occasion giving a feeling, "I am yours, just as before." Differences don't matter." I am for you, you are for me," should be the main feature in that function.

Hearts may meet again but the occasion which is over will not come back. One should not severe bonds from occasions which will not come back. If it happens, we come to regret, "We could not do what we ought to have done."

That regret will not help. It should not happen that one becomes close when relations are normal and distanced when they are strained.

NO NEED TO HIDE

We think we have two types of tastes... one which we like and the other we do under compulsion.

Can anyone make us do a thing which we don't like? No. Can others make us utter words which we don't like? No.

We bring down our own status by saying, "I am doing this for my livelihood. You think this is what I should be doing? What is my taste? What are my opinions? I am doing this work because I have no other choice." We shift the blame to someone else.

Who compelled us to do a job of killing our conscience? Certainly we select a means for our need which is convenient to us. Some people say, "Give me full freedom, I will show you what I am", as if they would achieve great things.

One director can make a film according to his intelligence. One writer can write according to his capacity. But to propagate that he can do better but is compromising because of people amounts to cheating one's own self.

So also a person in a profession can do the job according to his capacity. He is under illusion to think he has some hidden talents. Infact we can do what we can, and that is what we are doing.

No one in this world has the cleverness and capacity to imprison air and to oppress human talent.

TOO MUCH LOVE IS ALSO A HINDRANCE

Man lives because of freedom. Whether one has enough to eat or not a person has freedom to be good or bad. Only one-fourth of a human being lives on food. The remaining three-fourths he lives in freedom with content. If this ratio is disturbed it becomes imprisonment.

Can a parrot be happy in a golden cage? It does not like to be in captivity even when everything is provided. Outside it may be struggling to feed itself. Yet it has happiness in that. It has life in that. That is why irrespective of the salary no one likes to work without freedom. Human being cannot help but resist imposed restrictions.

One may be committing mistakes.He may be correcting them, he may be repeating them, yet he can live happily.

Even in the case of our own children more we impose restrictions, more they try to violate them. That is human nature. Every person can choose his own way.

He can decide how to live his life. Even if he is provided with everything saying, "This is how you can be secure. This is how your life can be smooth", he does not listen.

He would like to be free even if he had to do with one meal a day. That is why we wanted independence and won independence. Every person needs freedom and independence in everything. By nature man is a free man.

IT IS EASY TO TELL TRUTH

It is very difficult to lie in life. Because one has to remember what was said, when and to whom? If we have to tell the same people the comment we have passed, promises we have made and things we have praised how difficult it would be!

It is easy to tell truth. But we are making it topsy turvy in our life. We think telling lies is easy and to live by telling truth is very hard in this world. Under this illusion we create an untrue world and struggle in it.

Since truth is harsh some people may hesitate to have any dealings with us. They may think we are arrogant and never mince words.

One should not care for such opinion. Only a person with self confidence resorts to truth. A person who lacks it depends on untruth.

If we always speak truth there is no need to struggle to recall because we are clear about what we talk with whom. With a clear mind we can see everything as it is.

We should be transparent. In fact it is easy to be truthful. To lead a life of lies is like holding burning coals in the fist. Always one is chased by fear and anxiety.

A person with a nature that is truthful is always happy. A person who depends on truth is always successful. With this little principle called "truth" we can lead a peaceful life.

IT IS IN OUR ACTS

We love life. We fear death. But if we really love life, we can live as long as we want. But for that we are not doing certain daily activities.

We don't care for our body. Because of compulsion, we do certain things but are we giving adequate exercise and rest to the body? No. We eat whatever we please and get diseases.

When we know sweet is not good for our health, we continue to like it. When sour things don't suit us, we very much wish to eat them. It is a great example of strange mentality that we desire something which does not suit us.

Same is the case with our mind. Whatever comes to our mind, we do. We run after all wishes. We get tired in the process. We become weak and victim of illness. Then again we are afraid of death. We are not able to control our own body and mind. Infact there is no relationship between what we think and what we do. Bad habits and crooked mind will only throw us into the valley of death.

We can't say of an accident, but otherwise there is no need to fear our death. As long as we are discerning in our behaviour, only good things will happen.As long as we keep our body and mind intact and keep them in control, we need not fear untimely death.We can live as long as we please.

ALL ARE SELF-MADE

We have no power of choosing the country we have to be born in. We can't select in which religion, in which caste we are to be born. We don't even decide who should be our mother. These processes happen not taking into consideration our likes or dislikes.

Our quality, character or nature also is not made by us. To a great extent, we acquire these by birth.

Does that mean a bad person can never become good? Can't someone choose a good path from a bad path? Certainly he can.

Though we are not concerned with the good or bad that is within, we are free to choose the path we want. We can eliminate that devilishness within us and become human and good.There is a great opportunity in our hands to become divine from being mere human.

We are not remaining the same as we were at our birth. We are growing and developing physically and mentally. We are facing many evolutionary stages in life.We are responsible to change the results of evolution from bad to good. No one has a say in this.

If one is adamant to say, "Bad is my way," no one can do anything about it. On the contrary if we are determined, "Mine is a righteous path, whatever may be the difficulties I face, I will not give up truth and justice," and live up to this, we will certainly become divine. Our life will be an abode of peace.

There is no other prayer better than asking for a good mind.